Southern Scrumptious

HOW TO CATER YOUR OWN PARTY
BY BETTY BRANDON SIMS

For my family who has always been
in my heart and my kitchen.

Southern Scrumptious
How to Cater Your Own Party

Copyright© Betty Brandon Sims
4107 Indian Hills Road
Decatur, Alabama 35603
256-355-9738

Library of Congress Catalog Number: 97-92552
ISBN: 0-9659053-0-6

Edited, Designed and Manufactured by
Favorite Recipes® Press
an imprint of

FRP

P.O. Box 305142
Nashville, Tennessee 37230
800-358-0560

Project Manager: Charlene Sproles
Project Coordinator: Elizabeth Miller
Project Editor: Debbie Van Mol
Designer: Bill Kersey
Art Director: Steve Newman

Manufactured in the United States of America
First Printing: 1997 10,000 copies
Second Printing: 1998 10,000 copies

E-mail address: Mettysims@aol.com

Acknowledgements

To my husband, Dr. Bill Sims, and my children and their spouses, Libby and Carl Patrick, Sheri and Pete Hofherr, Tara and Bill Sims, and Lisa and Paul Wallace, who allowed me to realize a dream and supported me with love.

My sincere appreciation to my staff at Johnston Street Cafe who loyally gave of their time and hearts, and to my other friends who came when I most needed them.

Artists

Cover Illustration: Mitch Howell Coon

Mitch is a cover designer and illustrator from Hartselle, Alabama. She is primarily a watercolor portraitist, but has done a number of book covers and illustrations. Mitch, a Fine Arts graduate of Birmingham Southern College, has work represented in collections throughout this country and abroad. She is listed in the *Who's Who in American Art* and in the *International Who's Who* in Art and Antiques, and is a member of the Watercolor Society of Alabama.

Line Drawings: Lisa Sims Wallace

Lisa is my youngest daughter. She loves to cook, dabble in the arts, and celebrate life. She is a Pediatric Nurse Practitioner in Florence, Alabama, where she lives with her husband, Paul, and their sons, Paul, Jr. and Sims.

My sincere thanks to all who assisted me at FRP.
There could not be a nicer company with which to work.

Contents

Introduction

Catering Your Own Party in Southern Scrumptious *Style*

In the South, we love to entertain and you will find *Southern Scrumptious* menus and recipes to select from throughout this book that have been tested in a restaurant and catering setting, my own Johnston Street Cafe. Catering *your* own party can be a rewarding experience and one that does not have to be overwhelming. We want to take the fear out of entertaining for you. It truly can be fun! The key to successful entertaining is organization, as well as creativity. Make a guest list; select, purchase, and send invitations; and browse through our menus and select one that allows for some items to be prepared ahead. Make your grocery list early, and prepare and freeze these items. Lists and more lists are in order.

Entertaining has become more casual. Instead of always using the fine china and silver in the formal dining room, we are moving to more casual parties in the kitchen, or in the yard or on the porch for a cookout. Guests even take part in the cooking. Welcome your friends and family into your home informally, and allow everyone to relax.

Actually, when we have guests into our homes, the object is to get the people we care about together to share a meal and have a good time. I love to cook for my friends and family. Another real secret to successful entertaining is making your guests feel welcome. After spending ten years in the catering business, I realize, firsthand, how important it is to get things done ahead and stay very organized.

Keeping a simple diary of your home entertaining can provide distinct pleasure. This makes that party last, as you thumb back through your book through the years. Get a handsome book with blank pages. Fill the pages with what you find important. The occasion, your guests, and the menu are important, of course, but more important are the remembrances that make each occasion unique, such as a great story that was told, funny mishaps, etc. Give your parties names describing the events. Record place cards, flyers, etc., if you desire. You will be surprised how much fun these accounts will be to read over through the years.

Now, have fun with *your* catering!

Tips and Guidelines for Catering Your Own Party

- Plan the date, time, place, budget, and duration of the party. In your budget, keep in mind the cost of the party ingredients, rental equipment, hired help, flowers, beverages, invitations, and other incidentals.
- Plan a menu that can be executed perfectly by you. Don't be overambitious, or you will spend most of your time in the kitchen.
- Do all of the shopping early. Write out complete shopping lists, and cross off items as you find them.
- You can calculate how much to buy and cook for any size party by counting out portions. If you are having swordfish steaks, provide one per person (include 2 or 3 extra for the men for a party of 12). Count asparagus by the serving, allowing 8 spears per person. If you are having Garlic Mashed Potatoes, allow 1 medium potato per person. A handful of salad is a single salad size—a great realization. Allow 1½ rolls or pieces of bread per person.
- Don't be inflexible when it comes to your menu. If asparagus is unavailable, then look for an alternative.
- Do as much preparation in advance as possible. Go over each recipe so that you can plan an effective cooking schedule. Know which dishes can be prepared ahead and frozen.
- Set the table, make the centerpieces, and be sure the linens are ironed.
- Plan a dessert that can be made several days in advance.

- Before the day of the party, make a little work plan and timetable for yourself. Try to gauge how long each task will take, and try to keep to your schedule.
- Leave yourself plenty of time to shower. Leave sufficient time to dress and fix makeup.
- Delegate some of the chores to others. The bar is a good example. Make sure there are plenty of mixers, bar fruits, appropriate beverages, and ice, and let someone else attend to the drink-making. It takes time to open wine bottles, so even that must be written into the schedule.
- Have all the plates ready and in place—dinner plates, salad plates, and dessert plates. Warm the plates for hot food and chill the plates for cold desserts if you have them.
- Try to ease the burden of cleanup by filling a sink with warm soapy water for the dirty dishes and flatware as it is cleared from each course. Scrape the dishes as they are brought into the kitchen, and place in the sink. I rarely wash dishes while guests are present.
- Be relaxed and cheerful. Even if you experience delays in the kitchen, don't let your guests feel the tension.
- Serve everything at a leisurely pace and try to keep up with the conversation around you.
- If you are not a gourmet cook, keep it simple. Everyone will have a better time. Make and freeze an easy casserole ahead of time, and serve it with a salad, bread, and a dessert.

A Heart Warming

Brunch

Menu

Cold Spiced Fruit

Praline Bacon

Fancy Egg Scramble

Cheese Grits

Sour Cream Coffee Cake

Pecan Orange Muffins

Kir Royale

Orange Blush

French Hot Chocolate

Coffee Bar

If you want to have friends over for a casual inexpensive get-together, a mid-morning brunch is the right answer. It is one of my favorite ways to entertain brides, out-of-town weekend guests, football fans, etc. An easy beautiful centerpiece could be just oranges or lemons in a pretty crystal or oriental bowl studded with sprigs of boxwood between the fruit. Use china or the attractive, heavy paper plates. Wrap the silverware in linen or paper napkins and tie with raffia or ribbons. I prefer to serve buffet style. Line up your buffet table in this order: plates and silverware, water and kir royales on tray, cold spiced fruit, fancy eggs, bacon, muffins, and coffee cake (may be frozen ahead 2 or 3 weeks). You may want to seat guests at tables covered with bright cloths or guests may use lap trays, stack tables, or end tables.

The day before your brunch, make your spiced fruit, prepare your fancy eggs, and refrigerate. Make your muffins and coffee cake if you haven't already. The day of the party, pour kir royales just before serving, warm eggs, broil bacon, warm muffins and coffee cake. You may want to offer water on a silver tray along with kir royales and coffee. It is much easier if all the beverages are prepared in advance. Coffee can be held in thermal containers and the juice served in pitchers so that the guests may help themselves.

Cold Spiced Fruit

1 (20-ounce) can pineapple chunks
1 (16-ounce) can sliced peaches
1 (20-ounce) can pear chunks
1 cup sugar
1/2 cup plus 1 tablespoon vinegar
1 (3-ounce) package cherry gelatin
3 cinnamon sticks
5 whole cloves

Drain the pineapple, reserving 3/4 cup juice. Drain the peaches and pears, reserving 1/2 of the juice. Combine the pineapple, peaches and pears in a bowl and mix gently. Combine the reserved juices, sugar, vinegar, gelatin, cinnamon sticks and cloves in a saucepan. Simmer for 30 minutes, stirring occasionally. Pour over the fruit, tossing to mix. Chill, covered, for 24 hours, stirring occasionally. Discard the cinnamon sticks and cloves. This salad does not congeal but the gelatin keeps the liquid from being too thin. Use fresh fruit if in season.

Yield: 10 servings

Praline Bacon

1 pound (12 slices) thick-sliced bacon
3 tablespoons sugar
1 1/2 teaspoons chili powder
1/4 cup finely chopped pecans

Arrange the bacon in a single layer on a broiler rack in a broiler pan. Bake on the middle oven rack at 425 degrees for 10 minutes or just until the bacon begins to turn golden brown. Sprinkle with a mixture of the sugar and chili powder; sprinkle with the pecans. Bake for 5 minutes longer or until brown and crisp. Drain praline-side up on paper towels.

Yield: 6 servings

Plant Centerpieces

Blooming plants in small pots, arranged in a basket with a little moss tucked around the base of the plants, make a quick and attractive centerpiece.

Fancy Egg Scramble

1 cup (4 ounces) chopped
   baked ham
1/4 cup chopped green onions
3 tablespoons butter
12 eggs, beaten
1 (3-ounce) can mushroom
   stems and pieces, drained
1 recipe Cheese Sauce
2 1/4 cups (3 slices bread) soft
   bread crumbs
4 teaspoons melted butter
1/8 teaspoon paprika

Sauté the ham and green onions in 3 table-spoons butter in a skillet until the green onions are tender. Stir in the eggs. Cook just until set, stirring constantly. Fold the egg mixture and mushrooms into the Cheese Sauce in a bowl. Spoon into a greased 3-quart baking dish. Combine bread crumbs, 4 teaspoons butter and paprika in bowl and mix well. Sprinkle over prepared casserole. Chill, covered, for 30 minutes or longer. Bake, uncovered, at 350 degrees for 30 minutes.

Yield: 10 servings

Lemon Tea

Remove the rind from one lemon using a grater or zester and infuse with a black tea to make a delicious hot or cold lemon tea.

Cheese Sauce

2 tablespoons butter
2 tablespoons flour
1/2 teaspoon salt
1/8 teaspoon pepper
2 cups milk
1 cup (4 ounces) shredded
   sharp Cheddar cheese

Heat the butter in a saucepan until melted. Stir in the flour, salt and pepper until blended. Add the milk gradually. Cook until thickened and bubbly, stirring constantly. Add the cheese, stirring until melted. Or Sauce may be prepared in the microwave. Place butter in a 2-quart Pyrex cup. Microwave on High (100%) for 1 minute, or until melted. Whisk in flour, salt and pepper. Add milk gradually, whisking constantly. Microwave on High (100%) for 4 minutes, stirring or whisking at 2 minute intervals. Continue to microwave at 30-second intervals until of desired consistency. Add the cheese, stirring until melted.

Cheese Grits

6 cups water
1 teaspoon salt
1 1/2 teaspoons minced garlic
1 1/2 cups quick-cooking yellow
   grits
1 1/2 cups shredded Cheddar
   cheese

Bring the water, salt and garlic to a boil in a large saucepan. Add the grits gradually, stirring constantly. Cook for 4 to 5 minutes, stirring frequently. Remove from heat. Stir in the cheese. Let stand, covered, for 1 to 2 minutes or until of the desired consistency. Spoon into a serving bowl; sprinkle with additional Cheddar cheese.

Yield: 10 to 12 servings

Sour Cream Coffee Cake

1 cup chopped pecans
1/2 cup coarsely chopped
   raisins, dried apricots,
   dates or currants (optional)
1 tablespoon sugar
1 teaspoon cinnamon
2 cups flour
1 teaspoon baking powder
1/4 teaspoon salt
1 cup unsalted butter,
   softened
2 cups sugar
2 eggs
1 cup sour cream
1/2 teaspoon vanilla extract

Combine the pecans, raisins, 1 tablespoon sugar and cinnamon in a bowl and mix well. Sift the flour, baking powder and salt together. Combine the butter and 2 cups sugar in a mixer bowl. Beat at medium speed until light and fluffy, scraping the bowl occasionally. Add the eggs 1 at a time, beating well after each addition. Add the sour cream and vanilla. Beat at low speed until blended. Add the dry ingredients 1/3 at a time, beating just until blended after each addition. Spoon 1/2 of the batter into a buttered and floured 9-inch tube pan or bundt pan. Sprinkle with the pecan mixture. Spoon the remaining batter over the pecan mixture; smooth the top. Bake at 350 degrees for 1 hour. Cool in the pan on a wire rack. Invert onto a serving platter.

Yield: 8 to 10 servings

Pecan Orange Muffins

1/2 cup butter, softened
1 cup sugar
2 eggs
Grated peel of 1 medium
 orange
1 teaspoon baking soda
2 cups flour
1 cup plain yogurt or
 buttermilk
3/4 cup finely chopped pecans
1/3 cup freshly squeezed orange
 juice
1 tablespoon sugar

Beat the butter and 1 cup sugar in a mixer bowl until pale yellow and creamy, scraping the bowl occasionally. Add the eggs 1 at a time, beating well after each addition. Stir in the orange peel and baking soda. Fold in 1/2 of the flour and then 1/2 of the yogurt. Repeat the process with the remaining flour and yogurt. Fold in the pecans. Spoon into greased or paper-lined muffin cups, dividing equally. Bake at 375 degrees for 20 to 25 minutes or until the muffins test done. Drizzle the orange juice over the hot muffins; sprinkle with 1 tablespoon sugar. Cool in muffin cups. Serve with apple jelly and sliced ham or smoked turkey.

*Yield: 12 regular muffins, or
48 miniature muffins*

Orange Blush

4 cups orange juice
4 cups cranapple juice

Combine orange juice and cranapple juice in pitcher and mix well. Pour over ice in glasses.

Yield: 8 servings

Kir Royale

2 teaspoons crème de cassis
2 bottles Champagne, chilled

Spoon 1/4 teaspoon crème de cassis into 8 Champagne glasses. Fill each glass 2/3 full of Champagne.

Yield: 8 servings

French Hot Chocolate

2¹/₂ (1-ounce) squares baking
  chocolate
¹/₂ cup cold water
³/₄ cup sugar
¹/₂ cup whipped cream
Hot milk

Melt the chocolate in a double boiler over
hot water. Stir in the cold water. Cook for 4
minutes. Add the sugar. Cook for 4 minutes.
Cool to room temperature. Fold in the
whipped cream. Place 1 or 2 tablespoons of
the chocolate in each cup. Add enough hot
milk to fill each cup and mix well. May store
the cooked mixture in the refrigerator and add
whipped cream and milk at serving time.

Yield: 12 servings

Coffee Bar

*Instead of serving plain coffee, set up a coffee bar. Brew the coffee with
slivered almonds or strips of orange peel for added flavor. Set out
brandy or several of your favorite liqueurs, such as kirsch, Galliano,
Kahlúa, Triple Sec, Tia Maria, or amaretto, to stir into the coffee.
Offer sugar cubes, whipped cream, and grated chocolate, and serve
with cinnamon stick stirrers. Add strawberries or maraschino cherries
to garnish a cloud of whipped cream on top.*

An Afternoon
Tea Party

Menu

Cheese Straws

Fruited Tea Sandwiches

Johnston Street Cafe Chicken Salad in Chou Puff Pastry

Heart-Shaped Scones with Devonshire Cream

Cinnamon Pecan Logs

Lemon Tarts with Crystallized Violets

Almond Tea Punch

Hot Tea

Afternoon Tea Parties can be held to celebrate almost any event: retirement, baby shower, birthday, golden wedding anniversary, etc. Tea has become so popular of late and promises to be more so. My daughter, Libby, has an afternoon tea each year with her friend, Jane, in Atlanta. They invite all of their female friends for a gala afternoon of delectable goodies complete with hats, gloves, and a prize for the most outrageous hat. It's lots of fun and I always "cater" the event. We add a chutney cheeseball with wheat crackers, peppermint brownies, and cream cheese brownies to the menu I have included.

Tea is a pleasant surprise from the usual invitation. It is an easy way to entertain. Invite your friends over for either afternoon tea or the heavier menu, "High Tea," which makes dinner unnecessary.

Anna, 7th Duchess of Bedford, grew tired of the sinking feeling which afflicted her every afternoon about 4 o'clock. In 1840, she plucked up courage and asked for a tray of tea, bread, and butter and cake to be brought to her room. Once she had formed the habit, she could not break it and spread the custom among her friends.

Afternoon Tea

"Under certain circumstances there are few hours in life more agreeable than the hour dedicated to the ceremony known as afternoon tea. There are circumstances in which, whether you partake of the tea or not, the situation is in itself delightful."

Opening words of *The Portrait of a Lady* by Henry James. Afternoon tea is a delightful combination of fine tea, pretty and delicious sandwiches, and pastries—a truly social event.

High Tea

What you will find at high tea: a large table spread with a white cloth; a heavy brown Firestone teapot pouring tea strong enough, as they say, to trot a mouse on; a side of smoked ham, perhaps, or an egg and bacon pie; a generous wedge of cheese; a dish of tomatoes and a bunch of watercress; some savory dish like potted shrimp or even jugged kippers; scrambled eggs; bread and butter with pots of jam and honey; a plate of sandwiches; hot toasted tea cakes; and appetite-cutting cakes often baked from recipes unique to region, full of dried fruit, oatmeal, and ginger.

Cheese Straws

This is the very best recipe for cheese straws the South can offer. Frances Patrick, our daughter Libby's mother-in-law, shared this one with me. I was thrilled that by substituting butter with corn oil margarine the amount of cholesterol was reduced.

16 ounces New York State
    extra-sharp Cheddar
    cheese, shredded
2 cups corn oil margarine,
    softened
4 cups flour
1 tablespoon sugar
3/4 teaspoon cayenne
1/2 teaspoon baking powder
1/8 to 1/4 teaspoon salt

Beat the cheese and margarine in an electric mixer until blended. Sift the flour, sugar, cayenne, baking powder and salt together in a bowl. Add to margarine-cheese mixture and blend. Spoon into a cookie press. Pipe into straws onto an ungreased baking sheet. Bake at 350 degrees for 18 minutes or until light brown.

Yield: 200 cheese straws

Fruited Tea Sandwiches

16 ounces cream cheese,
    softened
1 (8-ounce) can crushed
    pineapple, drained
1/3 cup orange marmalade
3 tablespoons ginger preserves
    or chutney
1/2 cup chopped pecans
1/4 cup finely chopped green
    bell pepper
1 tablespoon minced onion
1/2 teaspoon celery salt
1/2 teaspoon onion salt
8 maraschino cherries,
    chopped
Sliced raisin bread, crusts
    trimmed
1/2 cup chopped pecans

Beat the cream cheese, pineapple, marmalade and preserves in a mixer bowl until mixed. Stir in 1/2 cup pecans, green pepper, onion, celery salt, onion salt and cherries. Cut the bread slices diagonally into halves. Spread with the cream cheese mixture; sprinkle with 1/2 cup pecans. Arrange the sandwiches on a serving platter. May use as a spread for crackers, gingersnaps or Bremner wafers.

Yield: 25 to 30 sandwiches

Helpful Tea Party Hints

- Begin with cold water when brewing tea.

- Never boil tea.

- To prevent bitter-tasting tea, remove tea bags after tea has steeped.

- When preparing iced tea for a crowd, vary the flavor by adding 6 ounces of frozen lemonade to 1 gallon of tea.

- Make ice cubes with leftover tea. These cubes added to a drink will not dilute the beverage.

Johnston Street Cafe Chicken Salad

8 chicken breast halves
1 medium onion
1 rib celery
1 carrot
1 tablespoon salt
3 cups chopped celery
2 cups mayonnaise
3/4 teaspoon white pepper
1/8 teaspoon cayenne
Salt to taste

Rinse the chicken. Combine the chicken, onion, 1 rib celery, carrot and salt with enough water to cover in a stockpot. Cook for 45 minutes or until the chicken is cooked through. Drain, discarding the broth and vegetables. Chop chicken, discarding skin and bones. Mix chicken, 3 cups chopped celery, mayonnaise, white pepper, cayenne and salt in bowl and mix well. Chill, covered, until serving time. Add 2 cans drained and quartered artichoke hearts and 1 tablespoon dried tarragon or 1/4 cup chopped fresh tarragon for variety.

Yield: 6 cups

When I was the proprietor of Johnston Street Cafe, we actually used boneless chicken tenders for the Johnston Street Cafe Chicken Salad. The chicken breast is almost as tender and not quite as expensive. Joyce Phenore, who made all of the chicken salad, must have mixed thousands of pounds of it in the ten years she has been employed at the Cafe.

Chou Puff Pastry

2 cups water
1 cup margarine
2 cups flour
1/2 teaspoon salt
8 eggs

Boil the water and margarine in a saucepan until the margarine melts. Remove from heat. Beat in a mixture of the flour and salt with a metal spoon until blended. Cook over medium heat for 1 minute, stirring constantly. Spoon into a food processor container. Add 4 of the eggs. Process for 30 seconds. Add the remaining 4 eggs. Process for 1 minute. Drop by teaspoonfuls onto 2 parchment-lined baking sheets. Bake each batch separately on middle oven rack at 425 degrees for 15 minutes. Reduce oven temperature to 375 degrees. Bake for 5 minutes. Make a slit in the top of each pastry. Reduce oven temperature to 350 degrees. Bake for 5 minutes longer. Fill the puffs with savory fillings such as shrimp paste and boursin cheese or with dessert fillings such as lemon curd and white chocolate mousse.

Yield: 60 small puffs

Heart-Shaped Scones

2¹/₂ cups flour
1 tablespoon baking powder
¹/₂ teaspoon salt
¹/₂ cup unsalted butter,
   chopped, chilled
¹/₄ cup sugar
²/₃ cup milk or whipping
   cream
Devonshire Cream

Mix the flour, baking powder and salt in a bowl. Cut in the butter with a pastry blender or fork until crumbly. Stir in the sugar. Add the milk, stirring with a fork until a soft dough forms. Shape into a ball. Knead on a lightly floured surface 10 to 12 times. Roll and cut with a heart-shape cutter. Arrange on an ungreased baking sheet. Bake at 425 degrees for 12 minutes. Remove to a wire rack to cool. Arrange on a serving platter. Serve with Devonshire Cream and your favorite jam in small crystal bowls.

Yield: 40 small scones

Devonshire Cream

1 cup sour cream
2 tablespoons sugar

Mix the sour cream and sugar in a bowl.

Yield: 1 cup

Cinnamon Pecan Logs

1 cup margarine
1 cup sugar
1 egg yolk
2 cups flour
2 teaspoons cinnamon
1 egg white, beaten
1 cup ground pecans

Beat the margarine and sugar in an electric mixer until creamy, scraping the bowl occasionally. Add the egg yolk, beating until blended. Stir in a sifted mixture of the flour and cinnamon. Spread over the bottom of a greased 10x15-inch baking sheet. Brush with the egg white and sprinkle with the pecans. Bake at 350 degrees for 15 minutes or until light brown. Let stand until cool. Cut into 1x4-inch logs. Remove from pan immediately. Do not substitute butter for the margarine.

Yield: 48 servings

Helpful Tea Party Hints

- Freeze fruit juice for ice cubes, add to tea and garnish with sprigs of fresh mint.

- Use simple syrup to sweeten large quantities of tea.

- When preparing larger quantities, allow tea to steep five minutes longer.

- When serving hot tea in a china cup, place a spoon in the cup. Pouring tea over the spoon helps avoid cracking the cup. The spoon absorbs the heat.

- For extra frosty iced tea, store glasses in the freezer for 30 minutes.

Lemon Tarts

Why stand and stir when you can "jet" around the kitchen doing other things as this lemon filling cooks in the microwave? Lemon curd may be kept for 3 weeks in the refrigerator. It's great to keep around to blend with whipped cream for a delicious cake filling or fresh fruit dip.

½ cup unsalted butter
1½ cups sugar
4 eggs
Juice of 3 lemons
1½ teaspoons grated lemon
 peel
1 recipe Tart Pastry Shells

Microwave the butter on High in a 2-quart Pyrex cup just until melted. Add the sugar, eggs, lemon juice and lemon peel and blend. Microwave on High for 4 minutes and whisk. Microwave on Medium-High for 4 minutes and whisk. Microwave on Medium-High for 4 minutes longer and whisk. Continue to microwave until thickened. Let stand until cool. Spoon into the baked Tart Pastry Shells.

Yield: 60 servings

Tart Pastry Shells

5 cups flour
2/3 cup sugar
½ teaspoon salt
2 cups cold butter, chopped
2 eggs
2 teaspoons vanilla extract
2 teaspoons lemon zest
 (optional)

Combine the flour, sugar and salt in a food processor container fitted with a metal blade. Add the butter. Pulse until of a coarse consistency. Add the eggs, vanilla and lemon zest. Process until the mixture forms a ball. Chill, wrapped in plastic wrap, in the refrigerator. Roll ⅙ inch thick on a lightly floured surface. Cut into rounds to fit miniature muffin cups. Fit the pastry into the muffin cups. Bake at 375 degrees for 10 minutes or until light brown. Pastry will continue to brown in the muffin cups after being removed from the oven.

There are few hours in life more agreeable than the hour dedicated to the ceremony known as afternoon tea.

—Henry James

Imagine how the world would be if everyone took a few moments to enjoy a cup of tea.

Crystallized Violets

*When the first violets unfurl their blossoms in April, I rush to pick
the most beautiful for candied violets...they are everywhere in our yard.
Rose petals and lilac florets also take well to crystallizing.*

Egg whites
Water
Violets
Superfine sugar

Beat the egg whites with a few drops of water in a bowl. Holding the violet by the stem, coat both sides of the petals with the egg whites using a paintbrush. Dip the petals in the sugar or sift sugar over the petals, shaking off the excess. Arrange on waxed paper. Let stand until dry; the larger violets may have to be turned with tweezers to allow them to dry completely. Snip off the stems. Store in an airtight container. The violets will keep indefinitely and can be used as garnish on cakes or other desserts.

Yield: Variable

Almond Tea Punch

3 lemons
4 cups water
2 cups sugar
2¹/₂ cups pineapple juice
2 cups strong tea
1 teaspoon vanilla extract
1 teaspoon almond extract
4 cups ginger ale, chilled

Squeeze the juice from the lemons into a bowl. Combine the lemon rinds, water and sugar in a saucepan. Bring to a boil. Boil for 3 minutes. Stir in the lemon juice, pineapple juice, tea and flavorings. Strain into a 4-quart container. Chill, covered, in the refrigerator. Stir in the ginger ale just before serving. Pour into punch cups.

Yield: 16 to 18 servings

A Perfect Cup of Tea

Any tea you choose must be correctly brewed. A few common errors can turn a fine cup of tea into a bitter disappointment. The following steps are crucial to properly brewed tea.

First, start with cold tap water that has run freely for a minute or two, becoming fully aerated. Air adds body to the taste of tea. Bring the water to a rolling boil in a kettle. Meanwhile, warm a china teapot...never use a metal one, as it alters the taste...by rinsing it with hot water.

Pour the boiling water over the tea you have selected. Brew for 1 minute or longer if you like your tea a bit stronger. Herb teas should brew for at least 3 minutes. Otherwise, you could wind up drinking tinted water.

A Baby Shower
For Couples

Menu

Crab Meat Mousse

Caesar Salad

White Chicken Chili

Sour Cream Corn Bread

Raspberry Brownies

Iced Tea

Beer and Wine

A caterer who is also the mother of four grown children is much in demand. Have food, will travel. I once jumped in my car loaded to the top with food for 50 and headed toward Atlanta and my daughter, Libby and Carl Patrick's, home. This was definitely an informal occasion with beer and wine served on the deck from galvanized tubs filled with ice. The tea was served from pitchers, and we used 14-ounce clear plastic cups for drinks. Our china plate and chili bowls were white "everyday" china. Silverware was wrapped with colored napkins tied with ribbon, to which a pacifier was attached. The buffet was out on the breakfast room table, chili being served from a huge earthenware container I had found in Santa Fe, the salad in a large lucite bowl, and the corn bread in a basket lined with a colorful linen towel. The centerpiece was an ivy topiary that we had picked up at the Farmers' Market. We attached small useful baby items with floral picks. You could use just one kind of flower such as lilies, glads, or tube roses in a clear crystal vase. Add to this centerpiece, silver baby cups, rattles, etc., or baby toys, such as stuffed animals and blocks. The entire house had balloons filled with helium, floating at ceiling-height with ribbons dangling.

More and more, baby showers are not just for women, but now include the proud father, his family, and friends. This particular party was to celebrate the soon-to-be arrival of the baby of my niece, Susan, and her husband, Phil Harrison. Presents for the new parents could be placed in a portable crib, which was given by the hosts, or a large ribbon-tied basket.

Crab Meat Mousse

*This recipe is for those people who cannot live without a
crab meat, salmon, or shrimp mousse.*

1½ cups chopped cooked crab
    meat or salmon
1 cup chopped celery
½ cup chopped green bell
    pepper
3 tablespoons lemon juice
2 tablespoons grated onion
1 tablespoon Worcestershire
    sauce
1 teaspoon salt
½ teaspoon Tabasco sauce
1½ tablespoons unflavored
    gelatin
⅓ cup cold water
1 (10-ounce) can tomato soup
9 ounces cream cheese
1 cup mayonnaise

Line mold with plastic wrap. Combine the crab
meat, celery, green pepper, lemon juice, onion,
Worcestershire sauce, salt and Tabasco sauce in
a bowl and mix well. Let stand to allow flavors
to blend. Soften the gelatin in the cold water
for 5 minutes and mix well. Combine the soup
and cream cheese in a double boiler. Cook over
low heat until blended, stirring frequently. Stir
in the gelatin mixture. Remove from heat. Cool
until slightly thickened. Stir in the mayonnaise.
Add the crab meat mixture and mix well.
Spoon into prepared mold. Chill until set.
Invert onto serving platter. Serve with assorted
party crackers. May serve as a salad. Substitute
shrimp for crab meat or salmon if desired.

Yield: 5 cups

*Small collections, such as
porcelain bunnies for
Easter or baby toys for a
baby shower, added to
the greenery are simple
ways to decorate.*

Caesar Salad

1 cup bread cubes
Olive oil to taste
Salt to taste
1 clove of garlic
1 tablespoon lemon juice
½ teaspoon dry mustard
Tabasco sauce to taste
3 tablespoons olive oil
2 bunches romaine, torn into
    bite-size pieces
½ cup freshly grated Parmesan
    cheese
1 can anchovies, drained

Toast the bread cubes in olive oil to taste
in a skillet until brown on all sides. Sprinkle
salt over the bottom of a large wooden salad
bowl. Rub with the garlic. Add the lemon
juice, dry mustard and Tabasco sauce to the
bowl, stirring with a wooden spoon until the
salt dissolves. Add 3 tablespoons olive oil
gradually, stirring until blended. Add the
romaine, tossing to coat. Sprinkle with the
cheese. Add the anchovies. Sprinkle with the
toasted bread cubes and toss gently with a
wooden fork and spoon.

Yield: 6 servings

White Chicken Chili

6 whole chicken breasts, split
1 large yellow onion, chopped
5 cloves of garlic, minced
6 tablespoons olive oil
2 red bell peppers, chopped
4 jalapeños, seeded, minced
2 tablespoons chili powder
1/8 teaspoon cinnamon
4 (16-ounce) cans Great
   Northern beans, drained
2 (28-ounce) cans chopped
   tomatoes, coarsely puréed
1 (8-ounce) can pitted black
   California olives, drained,
   sliced
1 (6-ounce) can tomato paste
1 cup beer
1/4 cup grated unsweetened
   chocolate
Salt to taste
Sour Cream
Shredded Cheddar cheese
Chopped scallions
Chopped avocados

Rinse the chicken. Combine the chicken with enough water to cover in a stockpot. Simmer for 45 to 60 minutes or until cooked through; drain, reserving the stock. Chop the chicken, discarding the skin and bones. Sauté the onion and garlic in the olive oil in a stockpot for 5 minutes. Add the red peppers and jalapeños. Sauté briefly. Add the chicken and enough of the reserved stock to make of the desired consistency. Stir in the chili powder and cinnamon. Add the beans, undrained tomatoes, olives, tomato paste and beer. Mix well. Simmer over medium heat for 30 minutes, stirring occasionally. Stir in the chocolate and salt. Ladle into chili bowls. Serve with sour cream, shredded Cheddar cheese, chopped scallions and avocados as garnish.

Yield: 16 servings

Sour Cream Corn Bread

1/4 cup margarine
1 cup cream-style corn
1 cup sour cream
1 cup self-rising cornmeal
1/2 medium onion, grated
  (optional)
2 eggs, beaten

Heat the margarine in an 8x8-inch baking pan or an 8-inch cast-iron skillet at 350 degrees until melted, tilting the pan to coat. Combine the corn, sour cream, cornmeal, onion and eggs in a bowl and mix well. Pour in the melted margarine and mix well. Spoon into the prepared pan. Bake at 350 degrees for 35 to 40 minutes or until brown. Add 1 can chopped jalapeños or 4 finely chopped jalapeños for a spicier corn bread. Decrease the fat grams by using light sour cream.

Yield: 8 to 10 servings

Raspberry Brownies

We added this brownie to our menu a couple of years ago. It has been a big hit!

8 ounces unsweetened
  chocolate
1 cup butter
1 cup margarine
4 cups sugar
8 eggs, beaten
2 cups flour
1 teaspoon salt
2 cups chopped pecans
1 1/2 cups raspberry preserves
Chocolate Glaze (at right)

Combine chocolate, butter and margarine in 2-quart microwave-safe dish. Microwave at half power until melted. Stir at 2 minute intervals. Combine sugar and eggs in bowl and mix well. Stir in chocolate mixture, flour and salt. Add pecans and mix well. Spoon into 11x13-inch baking pan coated with nonstick cooking spray. Bake at 350 degrees for 30 minutes. Spread with raspberry preserves. Let stand until cool. Spread with Chocolate Glaze. Cut into squares.

Yield: 12 large or 48 small brownies

Chocolate Glaze

2 cups chocolate chips
1 cup whipping cream

Microwave chocolate chips on Medium in a 2-quart Pyrex cup for 2 minutes or until melted. Add the whipping cream, whisking until smooth.

A Southern
Picnic

Menu

Sweet Broccoli Salad
Confetti Yam Salad with Cilantro
Honey Mustard Chicken
Angel Biscuits with Ham
Cream Cheese Brownies
Real Lemonade
White Sangria

*I*t's always fun to see what surprises the picnic basket holds. Picnics are about taking the time to pack something homemade into the cooler and finding a really nice location to share food with someone you love. Just remember the utensils, something to sit on, and the corkscrew for the wine—and if it doesn't rain, the day will be delightful. Picnic is from the French word *piquenique*, entered into the English language in 1748. It is derived from the word *picorer*, meaning to pick, peck, or scratch for food, and *nique*, meaning something small.

Prepare as much of this menu as possible the day before. The honey mustard chicken can be prepared a day ahead. Sauté the chicken, pour the marinade over, and refrigerate until the day of the picnic. Or, bake the chicken a day ahead, refrigerate, and let come to room temperature to serve. The broccoli salad, the yam salad, the angel biscuits with ham, and the sangria may be done the day before and refrigerated. Brownies may be made and frozen a week or so ahead. This picnic may be packed in a cooler and served from plastic containers on a tablecloth spread on the ground, or would do equally well on the backyard picnic table or at a tailgate party.

> *We are to walk about your gardens, and gather the strawberries ourselves, and*
> *sit under the trees . . . and it is all to be out of doors, a table spread in the*
> *shade, you know. Everything as natural and simple as possible.*
>
> —from *Emma* by Jane Austin

Picnic Packing Tips

- Pack chilled and unchilled foods separately—soggy cookies or chips are depressing.

- Double-wrap foods going into an ice chest. Zipper lock bags are indispensable—first wrap sandwiches in foil and then place in sealed bags for maximum dryness.

- Permanent frozen blocks are great for ice chests, as they don't make a mess as they melt. If using ice cubes, seal in zipper lock bags to prevent leakage.

- Wrap wine glasses and other breakables in cloth napkins. Any picnic worthy of wine and glassware is worth the price of some extra laundry.

Sweet Broccoli Salad

This salad always got rave comments whenever we served it at catering events or at Johnston Street Cafe. A unique combination of ingredients.

2 bunches of fresh broccoli
1/2 cup raisins
1/2 cup chopped pecans
1/2 cup chopped purple or red
   onion
1 recipe Apple Cider Dressing
12 slices bacon, crisp-fried

Break the broccoli into florets and chop some of the stems into small pieces. Mix the broccoli, raisins, pecans and onion in a salad bowl. Pour Apple Cider Dressing over the salad just before serving. Crumble the bacon over the top.

Yield: 8 servings

Apple Cider Dressing

1 cup mayonnaise
1/2 cup sugar
2 tablespoons apple cider
   vinegar

Mix the mayonnaise, sugar and vinegar in a bowl. Let stand, covered, in the refrigerator overnight.

Pansy (Johnny-Jump-Up)

The centers of pansies (Johnny-Jump-Ups) taste slightly like root beer or cinnamon. They are used primarily for color and as a textural contribution to salads, or as a garnish.

Confetti Yam Salad with Cilantro

My sister, Catherine Stainback in Atlanta, had this very different salad at a restaurant and kept going back to taste it. She was able to duplicate it almost exactly.

4 pounds fresh yams
Salt to taste
$^1/_2$ cup sliced green onions
$^1/_2$ cup chopped red bell pepper
$^1/_2$ cup chopped green bell
  pepper
$^1/_2$ cup chopped celery
$^1/_2$ cup chopped fresh cilantro
$^1/_4$ cup lemon juice
1 teaspoon salt
$^1/_4$ teaspoon pepper
$^1/_3$ cup vegetable oil
$^1/_2$ teaspoon grated lemon zest
1 tablespoon sugar

Cook the yams in boiling salted water to cover in a saucepan for 30 minutes or until tender. Drain and cool slightly. Peel and cube the yams. Combine with the green onions, red pepper, green pepper and celery in a large bowl. Mix the cilantro, lemon juice, 1 teaspoon salt, pepper, oil, lemon zest and sugar in a medium bowl. Pour over the vegetable mixture and toss. Chill thoroughly.

Yield: 8 to 10 servings

Honey Mustard Chicken

10 (6-ounce) boneless chicken
  breasts
Salt and freshly ground pepper
  to taste
2 tablespoons olive oil
$^1/_3$ cup Dijon mustard
$^1/_4$ cup olive oil
$^1/_3$ cup lemon juice
3 tablespoons honey
2 teaspoons minced fresh
  ginger

Season the chicken all over with salt and pepper. Heat 2 tablespoons olive oil in a large skillet over high heat. Add the chicken. Cook for 5 minutes or until the chicken is brown on both sides, stirring constantly. Arrange in a single layer in a foil- or parchment-lined roasting pan. Mix the Dijon mustard, $^1/_4$ cup olive oil, lemon juice, honey, ginger and additional pepper in a small bowl. Pour over the chicken. Bake, covered with foil, at 350 degrees for 30 minutes; remove the foil. Bake for 30 minutes longer. Let stand until cool before serving.

Yield: 10 servings

Picnic Table Setting

- DO use an outdoor festivity as an incentive to whip your porch, patio, yard, and garden into gorgeous summer shape. For centerpieces, consider live flowers and herbs that won't merely wilt and die, but will instead become beautiful and sentimental additions to your plant beds.

- DO furnish ample seating.

- DO attach linens to the tables with double-sided tape or pins in case of high winds.

- DO protect candles with votive or hurricane glass to prevent centerpieces and table linens from catching fire.

Angel Biscuits with Ham

2 envelopes dry yeast

$^1/_4$ cup warm water

5 cups flour

1 tablespoon baking powder

1 teaspoon baking soda

2$^1/_2$ tablespoons sugar

1 teaspoon salt

1 cup unsalted butter, cut into
small pieces

2 cups buttermilk

$^1/_2$ cup melted unsalted butter,
cooled

Thinly sliced cooked country
ham

Butter a baking sheet or line with parchment paper; set aside. Dissolve the yeast in the warm water in a small bowl. Sift the flour, baking powder, baking soda, sugar and salt into a large bowl. Cut in the butter until crumbly. Stir in the yeast and buttermilk. Turn the dough onto a floured board. Knead until smooth and elastic. Roll $^1/_2$ inch thick. Cut with 1$^1/_2$-inch biscuit cutter. Place the biscuits 2 inches apart on the baking sheet. Brush the tops with melted butter. Bake at 450 degrees for 10 to 12 minutes or until light golden brown. Split the warm biscuits in half and insert the ham. Angel Biscuits are also delicious sliced while warm, spread with an herb- or fruit-flavored butter, and filled with smoked turkey or smoked salmon.

Yield: 48 (1$^1/_2$-inch) biscuits

Picnic Table Setting

- DON'T wait until the last minute to work on your outdoor space. You may want to make color and fragrance adjustments in the days before the party.

- DO turn off your automatic sprinklers!

- DO spray in advance if ants, mosquitoes, or other pests might be a problem.

- DO provide plenty of shade. Seating arrangements under trees, gazebos, awnings, and tents are all tried-and-true options. A basketful of party-favor hats or visors commemorating the event is another heat-beating option.

Cream Cheese Brownies

1 cup unsifted flour
1 teaspoon baking powder
$^1/_2$ teaspoon salt
1 cup coarsely chopped
    walnuts
8 ounces semisweet chocolate
6 tablespoons butter
4 eggs
1$^1/_2$ cups sugar
$^1/_2$ teaspoon almond extract
2 teaspoons vanilla extract
6 ounces cream cheese,
    softened
3 tablespoons butter, softened
$^1/_2$ cup sugar
2 eggs
2 tablespoons flour
1 teaspoon vanilla extract

For the chocolate batter, mix 1 cup flour, baking powder, salt and walnuts together. Melt the chocolate and 6 tablespoons butter in a double boiler or microwave. Cool slightly. Beat 4 eggs in a bowl. Add 1$^1/_2$ cups sugar gradually, beating until well mixed. Add the chocolate mixture and mix well. Add the flour mixture and mix well. Stir in the almond extract and 2 teaspoons vanilla. For the cream cheese topping, beat the cream cheese and 3 tablespoons butter in a mixer bowl until smooth. Add $^1/_2$ cup sugar, 2 eggs, 2 tablespoons flour and 1 teaspoon vanilla and mix well. Pour $^2/_3$ of the chocolate batter into a buttered and parchment-lined 9x12-inch baking pan. Spread with the cream cheese topping. Spoon the remaining chocolate batter over the cream cheese layer. Swirl with a knife to marbleize. Bake at 350 degrees for 30 minutes or until a wooden pick inserted near the center comes out clean; do not overbake. Cool in the pan.

Yield: 12 large or 48 very small brownies

Real Lemonade

Remove the rinds from three lemons with a potato peeler. Place the rinds in a bowl with 1 cup sugar and 3$^2/_3$ cups boiling water. Leave the mixture to cool, then add the juice of the lemons and pour through a strainer. Serve well chilled.

White Sangria

$^{1}/_{3}$ cup fresh lemon juice
$^{1}/_{3}$ cup fresh lime juice
1 cup fresh orange juice
1 cup seltzer or club soda
$1^{1}/_{2}$ cups ginger ale
1 (750-milliliter) bottle dry
   white wine, chilled
$^{1}/_{2}$ cup Pimm's Cup (optional)
1 navel orange, cut into wedges
1 lemon, cut into wedges

Combine the lemon juice, lime juice, orange juice, seltzer, ginger ale, white wine, Pimm's Cup and half the orange and lemon wedges in a large pitcher and stir well. Add ice cubes. Serve with the remaining orange and lemon wedges.

Yield: 6 servings

Picnic Checklist

Things to Plan to Remember

- portable salt and pepper shakers
- corkscrew and can opener
- lemon or lime wedges for seasoning
- paper towels
- napkins
- serving spoons and knives
- plastic garbage bags for cleaning up

Picnic Necessities

- tablecloth and napkins with protective under sheet (a piece of plastic is great)
- a blanket or two
- bread knife and paring knife
- cutting board
- matches
- salt and pepper
- candles
- flashlight
- can and bottle opener
- paper towels, toilet paper, tissues
- small first aid kit, including sunscreen
- insect repellent
- plates, cups, utensils
- serving utensils
- jug of mineral water
- wet wipes for cleanup

Instant Picnic Foods

- pâté and hard sausages, such as salami
- cheese and crackers
- good bread
- fruit, especially berries and grapes
- olives
- focaccia
- boiled shrimp with cocktail sauce
- deviled eggs
- sushi to go
- Chinese barbecued duck, chopped into bite-size pieces
- cookies and brownies
- dolmades from the deli
- cracked crab

A Great
Grill – Out

Menu

Artichoke Rice Salad

Grilled Flank Steak on a Bed of Arugula Salad
or
Portobello Mushroom Burgers with Basil Mustard Sauce

Corn and Black Bean Salsa • Peach Salsa

Grilled Vegetables with Fresh Herbs

Corn Pudding

Garlic-Buttered French Bread
or
Summer Corn Bread

Banana Pudding

Grilled foods are becoming the centerpiece for many meals in every household. You don't need a special occasion to add some sizzle to your meals. Just fire up the grill and you, too, can have the ultimate no-fuss dinner or a backyard barbeque complete with wine, flowers, and music. Grill for your guests and cater your own party. Just be sure to eat grilled foods while they're hot and promptly refrigerate any leftovers. Remember, smoke cooking adds flavor to food, but it does not preserve it. Smoked food may take on a pink hue when fully cooked. To be sure that food is fully cooked, check the internal temperature with a meat thermometer and make sure the juices of all poultry and pork run clear.

The following menu can be prepared simply if you start a day or two ahead. The salad, sauces, artichoke rice salad, and the greens for the arugula salad may be done the day before. Also, cut up your veggies and grill them a day ahead if you like, refrigerating them until 2 hours before serving so that they are at room temperature. Then, the day of your grill-out, set the table, arrange placement of serving pieces, and grill flank steak and veggies if you did not prepare the vegetables earlier; if prepared ahead, be sure to let them warm to room temperature. Arrange fresh vegetables in a basket for an easy centerpiece. For convenience, use paper plates or everyday china and enjoy your no-fuss grill-out.

Grilling Tips

- Always preheat the gas grill or burn charcoal down to glowing coals. If you are using mesquite or other wood, soak the chunks for at least 30 minutes. Let the charcoal or gas fire get very hot, then add the wood and splash with water if it flares up. Keep a water sprayer handy in case you have a flare-up.

- Italian sausages are wonderful grilled as an appetizer. Prick the sausages all over and simmer in a saucepan of water for 10 minutes prior to grilling to be sure they are thoroughly cooked; pat dry. Grill until brown.

- A grill brush is a must. Use a long-handled, stiff wire brush for cleaning grill racks. Look for brushes with steel scrapers attached to the backside for removing burned on food bits.

- Much of the current grilling mania stems from the countless trendy restaurants stretching from coast to coast that have adapted the cooking method first popularized in California. It's a wonder there are any mesquite trees still standing.

- Marinate or lightly brush food with vegetable oil. This will help to keep food from sticking to the cooking grate.

- If using barbecue sauce, brush on during the last 15 to 20 minutes of grilling time.

- Place food on cooking grate with tongs or spatula. Using a fork will pierce food and precious natural juices will be lost.

- Never place cooked food on the same platter on which raw food was placed.

- Wash all platters and cooking utensils with warm soapy water.

- After removing food from the gas grill, close the lid and let residue burn off.

- Clean cooking grate with a wire brush or crumpled aluminum foil after every use.

- Foods on a crowded cooking grate require more time to cook than uncrowded foods.

- Using a timer will help to alert you when "well-done" is about to become "over-done."

More Grilling Tips

Always marinate meats, covered, in the refrigerator—never at room temperature. Marinating meat in a sealable plastic bag makes marinating and cleanup easy! Allow 1/4 to 1/2 cup of marinade for each 1 to 2 pounds of meat or fish, marinating for 2 to 8 hours. Discard leftover marinades that have been in contact with raw meat, fish or poultry. Do not reuse marinades. If marinade is to be used as a basting or dipping sauce, reserve a portion of the marinade before adding the raw foods.

Artichoke Rice Salad

2 (6-ounce) jars marinated
   artichoke hearts
2 cups chicken broth
1 cup rice
¼ cup chopped green onions
¼ cup sliced pimento-stuffed
   olives
½ cup mayonnaise
½ teaspoon curry powder
1 (8-ounce) can sliced water
   chestnuts, drained (optional)

Drain and slice artichoke hearts, reserving marinade. Bring the chicken broth to a boil in a saucepan. Stir in the rice. Simmer, covered, until tender. Cool slightly. Combine the rice, green onions, olives, artichoke hearts, reserved marinade, mayonnaise, curry powder and water chestnuts in a bowl and mix well. Chill thoroughly. May prepare one 8-ounce package chicken-rice mix to substitute for the chicken broth and rice.

Yield: 6 to 8 servings

Red Pepper Pods with Raffia

Create a Southwestern feel with red pepper pods tied together with natural raffia. Make a bow using several strands of the raffia; snip loops of the bow for the look of straw.

Arugula Salad

2 bunches arugula or watercress,
   separated
Cornichon Dressing
4 tomatoes, cut into ¼-inch
   slices
4 hard-cooked egg yolks, finely
   chopped
1 cup grated asiago cheese
Grilled Flank Steak (page 43)

Place the arugula in a salad bowl. Add the Cornichon Dressing and toss to coat. Arrange the sliced tomatoes over the top. Sprinkle with the egg yolks and cheese. Top with Grilled Flank Steak.

Yield: 6 servings

Cornichon Dressing

⅓ cup safflower oil
¼ cup rice wine vinegar
⅓ cup olive oil
2 tablespoons drained capers
4 cornichons (small pickles),
   chopped
3 tablespoons sherry wine or
   white wine

Combine the safflower oil, rice wine vinegar, olive oil, capers, cornichons and sherry wine in a jar. Cover tightly and shake to mix.

Grilled Flank Steak

¹/₂ cup red wine
¹/₄ cup chopped cilantro
1 clove of garlic, chopped
¹/₂ cup olive oil
1 small onion, chopped
Salt and pepper to taste
3 pounds whole flank steak

Combine the wine, cilantro, garlic, oil, onion, salt and pepper in a shallow pan and mix well. Rub into the steak. Marinate in the refrigerator for 2 hours or longer. Grill the steak to desired degree of doneness. Slice and serve over Arugula Salad (page 42).

Yield: 8 to 10 servings

Portobello Mushroom Burgers with Basil Mustard Sauce

1 cup mayonnaise
¹/₃ cup chopped fresh basil
2 tablespoons Dijon mustard
1 teaspoon fresh lemon juice
Salt and pepper to taste
¹/₃ cup olive oil
1 tablespoon minced garlic
3 red onions, sliced
6 (4- to 5-inch-diameter) portobello mushrooms, stems removed
6 (3¹/₂- to 4-inch-diameter) whole grain hamburger buns, split
6 large romaine leaves
6 large tomato slices

Soak 1¹/₂ cups mesquite chips in cold water for 1 hour. Mix the mayonnaise, basil, Dijon mustard, lemon juice, salt and pepper in a small bowl. Whisk the oil and garlic together in a small bowl. Heat the grill to medium-high heat (coals will turn white). Drain the chips and scatter over the coals. Brush both sides of the onion slices and mushroom caps with the garlic oil when the chips begin to smoke. Season with additional salt and pepper. Grill the onions and mushrooms for 4 minutes per side or until tender and golden brown. Remove the onions and mushrooms to a platter; cover with foil to keep warm. Grill the cut side of the buns for 2 minutes or until light golden brown. Place 1 half of a hamburger bun on each of 6 plates. Top each with 1 onion slice, 1 mushroom, 1 lettuce leaf and 1 tomato slice. Spoon some of the basil mustard sauce over the tomato slices. Top with the remaining bun halves. Serve the remaining sauce separately.

Yield: 6 servings

Corn and Black Bean Salsa

This colorful salsa is great with grilled meats.

1 (15-ounce) can black beans, rinsed, drained
1 cup frozen corn, thawed
¹/₂ cup chopped red bell pepper
¹/₂ cup chopped fresh cilantro
8 green onions, chopped
3 tablespoons lime juice
2 tablespoons balsamic vinegar
¹/₂ teaspoon ground cumin
¹/₄ teaspoon salt

Combine all of the ingredients in a bowl and mix well. Refrigerate in a covered container for up to 3 days.

Yield: 4 cups

Peach Salsa

1 (16-ounce) can peaches, drained
4 plum tomatoes, chopped
4 green onions, chopped
2 tablespoons chopped pickled jalapeño
1 tablespoon finely chopped fresh cilantro
1 tablespoon olive oil
1 tablespoon lime juice
1 teaspoon honey
1/4 teaspoon salt
1/4 teaspoon pepper

Combine all of the ingredients in a bowl, stirring gently. Refrigerate, covered, for up to 3 days.

Yield: 3 cups

Grilled Vegetables with Fresh Herbs

Andrea Chenault, an excellent cook and former manager, grilled tons of these.

8 red bell peppers, cut into halves
4 medium red onions, cut into quarters
12 small yellow squash (about 4 inches long), cut into halves lengthwise
12 small eggplant (about 4 inches long), cut into halves lengthwise
3/4 cup (or more) olive oil
1 teaspoon minced garlic (optional)
1 tablespoon minced mixed fresh herbs (basil, rosemary, thyme and chives)
Salt and freshly ground pepper to taste
Balsamic vinegar to taste

Cut the red pepper halves into quarters. Combine the red peppers, onions, squash and eggplant in a large bowl. Add the oil, garlic, herbs, salt and pepper and toss gently to mix. Grill in batches on a rack set 5 to 6 inches over glowing coals. Grill the red peppers and onions for 5 to 10 minutes or just until tender; grill the squash and eggplant for 10 to 15 minutes or just until tender. Remove to a platter to cool completely. Drizzle with balsamic vinegar. May grill 1 day ahead and store, covered, in the refrigerator. Bring the vegetables to room temperature before serving. May use any combination of vegetables. If using larger eggplant, cut into 1/4-inch-thick slices.

Yield: 10 to 12 servings

Corn Pudding

16 ounces fresh or frozen corn, or 1 (16-ounce) can whole kernel corn, drained
2 tablespoons (heaping) flour
1 tablespoon sugar
1/2 teaspoon salt
2 eggs, beaten
2 tablespoons melted margarine
1 1/4 cups milk

Mix the corn, flour, sugar and salt in a bowl. Add the eggs, margarine and milk and mix well. Pour into a baking dish set into a pan of hot water. Bake, covered, at 400 degrees for 30 to 40 minutes or until cooked through.

Yield: 6 servings

Summer Corn Bread

1 cup unbleached flour
1 tablespoon baking powder
3 tablespoons sugar
3/4 teaspoon salt
1 cup cornmeal
3 eggs
1 cup milk
3 tablespoons corn oil or
    melted butter
1 1/2 cups corn kernels (1 1/2 to
    2 ears)
2 fresh jalapeños, seeded,
    minced
1/3 cup minced red bell pepper
1/3 cup minced fresh basil
1/3 cup shredded Cheddar
    cheese

Mix the flour, baking powder, sugar, salt and cornmeal together. Beat the eggs in a large bowl. Beat in the milk and oil. Stir in the corn, jalapeños, red pepper, basil and cheese. Add the flour mixture, stirring just until blended; do not overmix. Spoon into a lightly greased 10-inch ovenproof skillet or 9x9-inch baking pan. Bake at 425 degrees for 25 to 30 minutes or until browned and cooked through. Cool slightly before serving.

Yield: 6 to 8 servings

Banana Pudding

Custards and sauces are so very easy in the microwave. This custard recipe is the one I use for so many things—trifles, bourbon sauce for bread pudding, and, of course, banana pudding.

1 cup sugar
1 teaspoon salt
1/4 cup cornstarch
5 cups milk
8 egg yolks, beaten
4 teaspoons vanilla extract
1 large package vanilla wafers
8 bananas, sliced
1 pint whipping cream,
    whipped
Toasted almonds

Mix the sugar, salt and cornstarch in a 2-quart Pyrex cup. Stir in the milk gradually. Microwave on High for 7 minutes or until slightly thickened, stirring every 3 minutes. Stir slightly more than half the custard into the egg yolks. Then whisk the egg yolk mixture into the custard in the Pyrex cup. Add the vanilla. Cool. Layer the vanilla wafers, bananas, custard and whipped cream in a 9x12-inch glass dish. Sprinkle with toasted almonds.

Yield: 8 to 10 servings

Garlic-Buttered French Bread

1/2 cup unsalted or lightly
    salted butter, softened
2 cloves of garlic, minced
Sliced French bread

Mix the butter and garlic in a bowl. Spread on the bread. Bake, wrapped in foil, at 350 degrees for 15 minutes.

Yield: Variable

A Sunday Night
Soup Supper

Menu

Goat Cheese, Walnut and Sun-Dried Tomato Spread with Crostini

Wilted Spinach and Bacon Salad

Portobello Mushroom Soup

Butter Braid Bread

White Chocolate Bread Pudding with White Chocolate Sauce

I love to entertain any night of the week with a "soup supper." A super soup meal would be an appetizer of Goat Cheese, Walnut and Sun-Dried Tomato Spread served with sliced apples, your soup du jour, a green salad, bread, and dessert, served casually from the stove, eaten in the kitchen, or before a roaring fire sitting on the floor around the coffee table—or use end tables or folding trays. Decorate the mantle with branches, a bird's nest, ivy, a vase of early daffodils, or magnolia leaves. Being a "southern touch," magnolias are flowers I use everywhere, just laying the small branches down the center of a table and using votive candles.

Your soup or stew could be made the day before and refrigerated for reheating the day of your get-together, as could your bread and dessert be made the day before. If you are pressed for time, buy a loaf of French bread from your favorite bakery and be sure to serve unsalted butter with it or olive oil flavored with a splash of balsamic vinegar. Set up a buffet on the breakfast room table and let guests serve themselves from the soup tureen or set up your buffet right in the kitchen next to the soup pot. You will have less to clean up if you serve soup directly from the pot, and your guests will like this casual approach. Use informal soup bowls that leave room for salad on the plate and colorful napkins. The main thing is that you have a truly delicious soup or stew and help your friends or family to relax and have fun.

If you really want to make it easy, buy brownies at the bakery for dessert. Serve with mint ice cream.

Goat Cheese, Walnut and Sun-Dried Tomato Spread

4 ounces goat cheese, such as
    Montrachet or a good chèvre,
    at room temperature
2/3 cup coarsely chopped
    walnuts or pine nuts
4 oil-packed sun-dried tomato
    halves, drained, coarsely
    chopped
1 large clove of garlic, coarsely
    chopped
1 teaspoon extra-virgin olive oil
1/4 teaspoon minced thyme
Salt and coarsely ground pepper
    to taste

Combine the cheese, walnuts, tomatoes, garlic, oil, thyme, salt and pepper in a food processor container. Process until mixed but slightly chunky. Spoon into a serving bowl. May place in a small bowl lined with plastic wrap and chill for 10 minutes or until firm. Unmold onto a serving plate and serve with crostini.

Yield: 8 to 10 servings

Wilted Spinach and Bacon Salad

This is delicious and one of my very favorite salads.

2 pounds fresh spinach
4 large button mushrooms,
    sliced
2 hard-cooked eggs, chopped
6 slices bacon
3 tablespoons brown sugar
3 tablespoons red wine vinegar,
    or to taste
Salt and pepper to taste

Trim the spinach to yield 1 pound. Rinse several times and pat dry. Combine with the mushrooms and eggs in a salad bowl. Cook the bacon in a skillet over medium heat for 15 minutes or until very crisp. Drain the bacon on paper towels. Strain the pan drippings through a fine sieve. Wipe out the skillet and pour in the drippings. Add the brown sugar. Cook over low heat until dissolved. Add vinegar, stirring well. Pour over the spinach mixture, tossing to coat. Top with bacon; season with salt and pepper.

Yield: 4 to 6 servings

This tangy spread pairs well with breadsticks or fruit, such as red or white seedless grapes, tart apples, Bosc pear slices, or kiwi wedges.

Portobello Mushroom Soup

2 leeks, white and pale green
    part only, chopped
1 medium onion, chopped
1/4 cup unsalted butter
10 ounces portobello
    mushrooms, chopped
1/2 cup flour
3 cups chicken stock or
    low-salt broth
2 cups half-and-half
1/4 teaspoon cayenne
Salt and freshly ground white
    pepper to taste
1/4 cup dry sherry

Sauté the leeks and onion in butter in a heavy saucepan over medium heat for 10 minutes or until tender. Add the mushrooms. Sauté for 5 minutes. Reduce heat to low. Add the flour. Stir in the chicken stock gradually. Simmer for 10 minutes or until thickened, stirring occasionally. Add the half-and-half. Simmer for 10 minutes longer. Season with the cayenne, salt and white pepper. Stir in the sherry. Simmer until heated through. Serve hot.

Yield: 6 servings

Butter Braid Bread

1 cup milk, scalded
1/2 cup butter
1/3 cup sugar
2 teaspoons salt
2 envelopes active dry yeast
1/4 cup warm water
3 eggs, beaten
6 to 7 cups flour
Melted butter
Poppy seeds or sesame seeds
1 egg white, beaten

Pour milk over butter, sugar and salt in a large bowl. Let stand until lukewarm. Dissolve yeast in warm water. Stir into the cooled milk mixture. Add eggs and 3 cups of the flour. Beat until smooth. Stir in enough remaining flour to make a stiff dough. Knead on a lightly floured surface until smooth and elastic. Place in a greased bowl; turn to coat surface. Let rise, covered, in a warm place until doubled in bulk. Divide dough into halves. Cut each half into 3 equal portions. Shape into 18-inch-long ropes. Braid 3 of the ropes together for each loaf. Place on a baking sheet. Brush with melted butter and sprinkle with the seeds. Let rise until doubled in bulk. Brush with mixture of egg white and water. Bake at 375 degrees for 30 to 35 minutes or until golden brown, brushing with butter after baking for 20 minutes.

Yield: 2 loaves

White Chocolate Bread Pudding with White Chocolate Sauce

1 loaf French bread
   (2¹/₂x10-inch), cut
   into 8 slices
2 cups heavy cream
¹/₂ cup milk
¹/₄ cup sugar
9 ounces white chocolate,
   chopped
1 egg
4 egg yolks
Semisweet chocolate, grated
   (optional)

Preheat the oven to 250 degrees. Place the bread slices on the middle rack. Heat for 20 minutes or until dry. Combine 1¹/₂ cups of the cream with the milk and sugar in a heavy saucepan. Heat until the sugar is dissolved, stirring frequently. Add 5 ounces of the chocolate. Simmer until melted, stirring constantly; remove from the heat. Whisk the egg and egg yolks in a bowl. Add the chocolate mixture gradually, whisking constantly. Tear the dried bread into 1-inch pieces. Add to the chocolate mixture, stirring well. Let stand for 1 to 2 hours or until the custard has been absorbed by the bread. Pour into a 2-inch-deep, 8-inch-square baking pan. Place the baking pan in a slightly larger pan and add hot water to come halfway up the sides of the baking pan. Bake at 350 degrees for 45 to 50 minutes or until the custard is set and the top is golden brown. Cool. Heat the remaining ¹/₂ cup cream in a small pan. Add the remaining 4 ounces of chocolate. Simmer until chocolate is melted, stirring frequently. Pour over the pudding. Sprinkle with grated semisweet chocolate.

Yield: 6 servings

Chocolate Leaves

Choose nontoxic leaves. (Rose, mint, and camellia are good choices.) Wash them in cold, soapy water; rinse and dry well. Melt 1 ounce semisweet chocolate according to package directions. Using a small, clean paintbrush, paint a thin layer of melted chocolate on the bottom side of each leaf. Set aside until firm. Repeat procedure 2 more times. Store chocolate-covered leaves in the refrigerator until the chocolate hardens or until ready to use. Starting at the stem ends, gently pull leaves away from the chocolate.

A Supper Club
Patio Party

Menu

Cold Zucchini Soup with Fresh Dill

Sauerkraut Salad

German Potato Salad

Butter Bean Salad

Oven-Roasted Barbecued Brisket on Buns

White Chocolate Brownies

Beaujolais

Tea Punch

*E*ntertaining is a celebration of sharing good food and drink with family and friends. There are many supper clubs in Decatur and the participants often have a terrace or patio dinner at a member's home.

Locate a colorful quilt or checkered cloth for the food table, festive napkins and a bunch of flowers or fresh fruit or veggies in a basket for the centerpiece. Use clear fold overs, casual china, or small baskets lined with a napkin. (With this menu you could not use baskets since you would need to cut the beef.) Fold overs or bakery boxes may be tied with ribbons or raffia, and they may even contain silverware and a covered cup of cold soup. This arrangement makes it easy on the hostess since the boxes may be stacked on the food table to be picked up by the guests. Serve tea from pitchers, or cold drinks iced down in a wheelbarrow. Provide more tables covered with quilts, or spread quilts on the ground or even hay bales for people to sit on. Provide Off and be sure to spray the lawn with Yard Guard an hour or so before the party.

Use baskets and big lucite bowls to serve from if you prefer not to serve in individual boxes or small baskets. This is one of my favorite menus since everything can be done the day before—even the grilled beef, which is very tender and is easily cut. If you grill it the day before, refrigerate when it cools. The day of the party, remove from refrigerator a couple of hours before serving. Slice and serve room temperature with bernaise sauce or mustard caper sauce. Be sure and make your grocery list early in the week and your organizational task timetable. A menu for a basket picnic might be a chicken salad or a roast beef croissant, Butter Bean Salad, Marinated Carrots (page 148), and a Chocolate Chubbie cookie (page 158).

Cold Zucchini Soup

1 onion, finely minced
1/4 cup butter
3 to 4 medium zucchini,
  unpeeled, sliced
3 1/2 cups chicken stock or
  broth
Salt to taste
1/2 teaspoon soy sauce
1/2 cup half-and-half

Sauté the onion in butter in a medium saucepan until translucent. Add the zucchini and chicken stock. Simmer over medium heat until the zucchini is tender. Pour into a food processor container. Process until puréed. Return to the saucepan. Stir in the salt, soy sauce and half-and-half. Pour into a bowl. Chill, covered, in the refrigerator.

Yield: 4 servings

Sauerkraut Salad

Great served as a condiment or as a side salad. You will not recognize the sauerkraut. Serve on a bun with beef.

1 3/4 cups sugar
1 cup white vinegar
1 cup chopped onion
1 cup chopped celery
1 cup chopped green bell
  pepper
1 cup chopped red bell pepper
1 cup chopped stuffed olives
1 (29-ounce) can sauerkraut,
  drained, rinsed
1 (14-ounce) can bean sprouts
  (optional)

Combine the sugar and vinegar in a saucepan. Bring to a boil; remove from the heat and let stand to cool. Mix the onion, celery, bell peppers, olives, sauerkraut and bean sprouts in a large glass bowl. Pour the cooled vinegar mixture over the vegetables, tossing to coat. Chill before serving.

Yield: 10 to 12 servings

Apple Blossoms

Light pink and white apple blossoms offer fresh fragrance and a slightly floral taste which complements salads and soups. Make sure the blossoms come from trees that have not been sprayed.

55 | *A Supper Club Patio Party*

Tea Punch

2 family-size tea bags
2 cups sugar
1 (12-ounce) can frozen
 orange juice concentrate
1 (12-ounce) can frozen
 lemonade concentrate
Sprigs of fresh mint

Brew the tea using package
directions. Pour into a
1-gallon container. Add
the sugar, orange juice
concentrate, lemonade
concentrate and enough
water to fill the container,
or add other juices such as
pear, peach, pineapple or
apricot. Stir well. Serve
over crushed ice. Garnish
with mint sprigs.

Yield: 1 gallon

German Potato Salad

*This potato dish is really good served with pork tenderloin and is
a great accompaniment to a hot sandwich.*

8 large potatoes, boiled,
 sliced
1 pound bacon
2 medium onions, chopped
3/4 cup packed brown sugar
1/2 cup vinegar
1/4 cup flour
2 cups water
1/2 teaspoon salt

Place the potatoes in a 9x12-inch dish. Fry the
bacon and onions in a skillet until the bacon
is browned and crispy. Remove the bacon and
onions to paper towels to drain, reserving the
pan drippings. Sprinkle the brown sugar into
the reserved pan drippings. Cook over low
heat until the mixture is thickened, stirring
constantly. Add the vinegar. Simmer until the
sugar is dissolved, stirring frequently. Stir in the
flour and enough water to make a thick sauce.
Simmer for 15 minutes, stirring frequently.
Season with the salt. Pour over the sliced
potatoes. Crumble the bacon over the potatoes.
Serve warm or at room temperature.

Yield: 8 to 10 servings

Butter Bean Salad

New and different—so good.

1 pound lima beans
1 red onion, minced
1 cup mayonnaise
2 teaspoons grated white
 horseradish
1 teaspoon Worcestershire sauce
2 tablespoons lemon juice
1/2 teaspoon salt
Dash of Tabasco sauce
1 teaspoon crumbled fresh
 rosemary
3 slices bacon, crisp-fried,
 crumbled

Cook the lima beans in water to cover in a
saucepan until the beans are tender. Drain
and rinse under cold water. Spoon into a
large bowl. Combine the onion, mayonnaise,
horseradish, Worcestershire sauce, lemon juice,
salt, Tabasco sauce, rosemary and crumbled
bacon in a small bowl; mix well. Pour over the
lima beans, stirring gently to coat. Chill,
covered, until serving time. May use fresh or
frozen lima beans.

Yield: 6 servings

Oven-Roasted Barbecued Brisket

This is one of my favorite entertaining menus since everything can be done ahead.
Serve on deli buns with Sauerkraut Salad (page 55) as a condiment on the bun.

6 pounds beef brisket or
   shoulder roast
1 teaspoon seasoned salt
1/2 teaspoon celery salt
1/2 teaspoon garlic salt
1/2 teaspoon onion salt
Pepper to taste
4 ounces liquid smoke
2 tablespoons Worcestershire
   sauce
1 cup Barbecue Sauce
   (at right)

Coat the brisket with the seasoned salts, pepper and liquid smoke. Cover with foil and place in the refrigerator overnight. Remove the foil. Sprinkle the brisket with Worcestershire sauce. Wrap tightly in foil and place in a baking pan. Bake at 250 degrees for 5 hours. Uncover and baste generously with the barbecue sauce. Bake for 1 hour longer. Cool slightly, then refrigerate. Skim off and discard the fat. Slice thinly or pull apart. Wrap in foil and chill until serving time. This freezes well.

Yield: 10 to 12 servings

White Chocolate Brownies

A very rich brownie that requires no frosting.

1 cup unsalted butter
10 ounces white chocolate,
   broken into small pieces
1 1/4 cups sugar
4 large eggs, beaten
1 tablespoon vanilla extract
2 cups unbleached flour
1/2 teaspoon salt
1 cup coarsely chopped pecans

Melt the butter and chocolate in a heavy saucepan over low heat, stirring until smooth. Remove from the heat. Stir in the sugar with a wooden spoon. Whisk in the eggs and vanilla. Add the flour, salt and pecans, stirring to moisten. Line a 9x11-inch baking pan with foil, leaving a 1-inch overhang of foil around the edge of the pan. Butter the foil. Pour the batter into prepared pan. Bake at 325 degrees for 30 to 35 minutes or until lightly browned; do not overbake. Let cool to room temperature. Chill for 3 hours before serving. Lift the brownies from the pan using the foil. Cut into 20 to 25 squares.

Yield: 20 to 25 brownies

Barbecue Sauce

1 medium onion, chopped
3 tablespoons catsup
2 tablespoons vinegar
1 tablespoon lemon juice
2 tablespoons
   Worcestershire sauce
1/4 cup water
1 teaspoon paprika
3 tablespoons brown sugar
1 teaspoon salt
1 teaspoon chili powder
1/2 teaspoon ground red
   pepper
1 teaspoon dry mustard
1/2 cup margarine

Mix all of the ingredients in a saucepan. Simmer for 5 minutes. Use as a sauce for chicken, beef or lamb.

Yield: 1 cup

A Buffet Dinner
With Friends

Menu

Marinated Goat Cheese with Fresh Basil

Fresh Strawberry Tossed Salad

Pork Tenderloin with Honey Sesame Marinade

Gruyère Cheese Grits

Sweet and Sour Green Beans

Cheese Scones with Herb-Seasoned Butter

Crumbly Pear Pie

Coffee Bar (page 15)

This is my daughter Lisa's favorite menu when she and husband, Paul Wallace, have friends over for dinner. A buffet dinner is the easiest way to serve guests. The day before your dinner, arrange serving pieces on buffet and set table. Marinated Goat Cheese may be made several days ahead as may be Mustard Caper Sauce. Early in the day prepare your pork tenderloin for baking if you like and make your Cheese Scones, cut out, and refrigerate. Poppy Seed Dressing for the salad may be prepared the day before and the greens washed and stored with a paper towel in a ziplock bag. Your pie can be made the day before and reheated just before serving. The day of your dinner, finish the meat, make your grits and Sweet and Sour Green Beans. Bake your grits and cheese scones just before serving. Arrange your food on your buffet so that guests may serve themselves. Use soft votives and Jackson vine with a variety of candlesticks and candles interspersed with the low votives, and perhaps a favorite small collection of porcelain tucked among the greenery.

Marinated Goat Cheese with Fresh Basil

8 (2- to 3-ounce) rounds goat
    cheese
1½ cups extra-virgin olive oil
4 bay leaves
1½ tablespoons thyme
1 tablespoon mixed white,
    black and green peppercorns
3 large cloves of garlic, slivered
3 tablespoons slivered fresh
    basil
Sliced French bread or crostini

Arrange the goat cheese in a single layer without touching in a shallow dish. Combine the olive oil, bay leaves, thyme and peppercorns in a saucepan and mix well. Cook until the mixture begins to sizzle and pop. Pour over the goat cheese. Sprinkle with the garlic slivers and basil. Chill, covered, for 8 to 10 hours. Discard the bay leaves. Serve at room temperature with French bread or crostini.

Yield: 24 servings

Fresh Strawberry Tossed Salad

2 heads romaine, torn into
    bite-size pieces
2 cups sliced fresh strawberries
²/3 cup pecans, toasted
4 ounces bacon, crisp-fried,
    crumbled
Poppy Seed Dressing

Toss the romaine, strawberries, pecans and bacon in a bowl just before serving. Add the Poppy Seed Dressing, tossing to coat. Spoon into a crystal salad bowl.

Yield: 8 to 10 servings

Borage

Borage is very nice sprinkled in salads. It is a deep blue, star-shaped, fuzzy flower with a hint of cucumber in the taste. Remove the fuzzy part and use the whole blossom. It is often used for tea-making.

Poppy Seed Dressing

3/4 cup sugar
1/3 cup vinegar
1/3 cup salad oil
1/3 cup chopped mild onion
1/2 teaspoon dry mustard
2 tablespoons poppy seeds

Combine the sugar, vinegar, salad oil, onion and dry mustard in a food processor container. Process until blended. Add the poppy seeds. Process just until mixed.

Pork Tenderloin with Honey Sesame Marinade

3 (³/4-pound) boneless pork
   tenderloins
¹/2 cup soy sauce
4 cloves of garlic, sliced
1 (2-inch) piece gingerroot,
   peeled, thinly sliced
¹/2 cup honey
1 cup sesame seeds, lightly
   toasted
Mustard Caper Sauce

Arrange the tenderloins in a shallow dish. Combine the soy sauce, garlic and gingerroot in a bowl and mix well. Pour over the pork, turning to coat. Marinate, covered, in the refrigerator for 2 hours, turning several times. Drain and pat dry. Spread the honey on a plate; roll the tenderloins in the honey. Spread the sesame seeds on a sheet of foil. Roll the tenderloins in the sesame seeds until coated on all sides. Place the tenderloins in a roasting pan lined with parchment paper or foil. Roast at 400 degrees for 25 minutes. Let stand for 5 minutes. Slice and serve with Mustard Caper Sauce.

Yield: 10 servings

Mustard Caper Sauce

1¹/2 cups mayonnaise
¹/2 cup sour cream
1 small jar capers, drained
3 tablespoons white wine
2 tablespoons Dijon mustard
¹/2 teaspoon white pepper

Combine mayonnaise, sour cream, capers, white wine, Dijon mustard and white pepper in a bowl and mix well. Chill, covered, in refrigerator. May substitute light sour cream and low-fat mayonnaise for the sour cream and mayonnaise.

Yield: 2¹/2 cups

Gruyère Cheese Grits

4 cups milk
1 cup grits
1/2 cup butter
1 egg, beaten
1 teaspoon salt
1/2 teaspoon ground white pepper
1/3 cup butter
4 ounces Gruyère cheese, grated
1/2 cup freshly grated Parmesan cheese

Bring the milk to a boil in a saucepan over medium heat, stirring frequently. Add the grits and 1/2 cup butter and mix well. Cook for 5 minutes or until of the consistency of oatmeal, stirring constantly. Remove from heat. Add a small amount of the hot mixture to the egg; add the egg to the hot mixture. Stir in the salt and white pepper. Add 1/3 cup butter and the Gruyère cheese and mix well. Spoon into a greased 2-quart baking dish. Sprinkle with the Parmesan cheese. Bake at 350 degrees for 1 hour.

Yield: 10 servings

Sweet and Sour Green Beans

This is so quick and delicious and can be served with many different menus. A real "find."

1 medium onion, chopped
1/2 cup bacon drippings
2 quarts cooked green beans, preferably large flat beans
1 cup vinegar
1 cup sugar
10 slices crisp-fried bacon, crumbled

Sauté the onion in the bacon drippings in a skillet until tender; drain. Combine the onion, green beans, vinegar and sugar in a saucepan and mix well. Simmer for 10 minutes, stirring occasionally. Add the crumbled bacon and mix well. Spoon into a serving bowl.

Yield: 10 to 12 servings

These grits are very creamy and cooked in milk. This is a little different version of the usual cheese grits recipe.

Cheese Scones

1¹/2 cups flour
1¹/2 teaspoons cream of tartar
1 teaspoon dry mustard
¹/2 teaspoon baking soda
¹/2 teaspoon salt
¹/4 cup unsalted butter or
   margarine, chopped, chilled
1 cup shredded sharp Cheddar
   cheese
2 tablespoons grated Parmesan
   cheese
¹/2 cup milk
1 egg

Combine the flour, cream of tartar, dry mustard, baking soda and salt in a bowl and mix well. Cut in the butter with a pastry blender or fork until crumbly. Add the Cheddar cheese and Parmesan cheese and toss to mix. Beat the milk and egg in a bowl with a fork until blended. Pour over the flour mixture, stirring with a fork until an easily managed dough is formed. Knead on a lightly floured surface for 10 to 12 times. Divide the dough into 2 equal portions. Knead each portion into a ball. Pat or roll each portion into a 6-inch circle. Cut each circle into 6 wedges. Arrange on an ungreased baking sheet. Bake at 400 degrees for 12 to 15 minutes or until medium brown. Cool, loosely wrapped in a tea towel, on a wire rack. May substitute 1¹/2 teaspoons baking powder for mixture of cream of tartar and baking soda. May roll the dough and cut with a biscuit cutter. I make these scones in the processor—just process the cold butter into the dry ingredients. Add cheeses and liquid and process just until blended. Knead lightly and follow above directions.

Yield: 12 scones

Herb-Seasoned Butter

1 cup lightly salted butter,
   softened
1 sprig of parsley, minced
1 sprig of thyme, minced
1 sprig of chervil, minced
1 sprig of dillweed, minced
1 sprig of tarragon, minced
Minced fresh chives
1/4 teaspoon freshly ground
   pepper

Beat the butter in a mixer bowl until light and
fluffy, scraping the bowl occasionally. Stir in
the parsley, thyme, chervil, dillweed, tarragon,
chives and pepper. Serve with Cheese Scones or
Cheese Herb Biscuits (page 72).

Yield: 1 cup

Crumbly Pear Pie

A super recipe from Peggy Burkhart who lives in the rolling hills of Kentucky.
Peggy and I have been exchanging recipes for a long time. We date back to
when ground beef could be purchased for forty-nine cents a pound.
The mace adds just the right touch to this recipe and should not be omitted.

1/2 cup sugar
3 tablespoons lemon juice
1 teaspoon grated lemon peel
8 medium pears, peeled, sliced
1 unbaked (9-inch) pie shell
1/2 cup flour
1/2 cup sugar
1/2 teaspoon ginger
1/2 teaspoon cinnamon
1/4 teaspoon nutmeg
1/4 teaspoon mace
1/3 cup butter

Combine 1/2 cup sugar, lemon juice and lemon
peel in a bowl and mix well. Add the pears,
tossing to coat. Arrange the pears in the pie
shell. Combine the flour, 1/2 cup sugar, ginger,
cinnamon, nutmeg and mace in a bowl and mix
well. Cut in the butter until the mixture is
crumbly. Sprinkle over the prepared layer. Bake
at 400 degrees for 35 to 40 minutes or just
until the pears are tender. Serve warm with
cinnamon ice cream if you can find it.

Yield: 8 servings

Candle Centerpieces

*Votive candles nestled
among Jackson vine makes
a simple table centerpiece or
use brass candlesticks
and candles with the
Jackson vine or ivy. Ribbon
curled down the center of
the table among the
greenery could pick up the
colors you are using.*

A Celebration
Of Spring

Menu

The Southern Mint Julep

Cream of Squash Soup with a Hint of Curry

Stuffed Fillet of Beef Tied with Leek Ribbons

Blanched Asparagus with Hollandaise

Wild Mushroom Soufflé

Carrot Purée

Cheese Herb Biscuits

Roasted Garlic Spread

Coconut Crème Brûlée

Cabernet Sauvignon

A spring dinner party request came often when I asked for suggestions for cooking classes at Johnston Street Cafe. Pull out the fine china, arrange the roses to go between the candlelight, press the linens, and get ready to celebrate. The soup, brûlée, and the asparagus may be done a day ahead and refrigerated. Vegetables may be chopped for the Stuffed Fillet. Set your table the day before and cut or buy your roses. As much as a week ahead, make your grocery list and think about a timetable for the day of the party. Cheese Straws (page 19) may also be served with wine or mint juleps before dinner.

On the day of your dinner, prepare your mushroom soufflé, except for folding in the egg whites, which needs to be done right before baking. The day of your dinner you can also make your mint julep syrup. Also, prepare your hollandaise sauce and keep it warm in a thermos until serving time. Cook your carrots and purée them, keeping this dish warm by placing the bowl over a pan of boiling water. Herb biscuits are made quickly any time during the day. They may be held unbaked in the refrigerator and baked just before serving. If you serve buffet style, you might serve the soup from small Jefferson cups from a tray in the living room before you invite your guests to the table—no spoons are required. Line up your buffet in this order—asparagus, beef, mushroom soufflé, carrot purée, and biscuits. Serve everyone's dessert after the dishes are cleared.

The Southern Mint Julep

3 tablespoons sugar
2 tablespoons water
8 fresh mint leaves
Finely crushed or shaved ice
3/4 cup Kentucky bourbon
4 fresh mint sprigs

Combine the sugar and water in a saucepan. Cook over low heat until the sugar dissolves, stirring occasionally. Remove from heat. Crush the mint leaves into the sugar syrup using the back of a spoon; mix well. Fill 4 tall glasses with crushed ice. Pour the mint syrup into the glasses, dividing equally. Pour 3 tablespoons bourbon into each glass. Top with a mint sprig. Let the mint syrup stand for 30 minutes for a stronger mint flavor.

Yield: 4 servings

Cream of Squash Soup with a Hint of Curry

1 large onion, minced
2 cloves of garlic, minced
1/4 cup melted butter or margarine
2 tablespoons vegetable oil
3 pounds yellow squash, thinly sliced
3 1/2 to 4 cups chicken broth
1 cup half-and-half
1 1/2 teaspoons salt
1/2 teaspoon white pepper
Chopped fresh parsley
1/2 teaspoon curry powder

Sauté the onion and garlic in a mixture of the butter and oil in a heavy saucepan until tender. Stir in the squash and chicken broth. Simmer, covered, for 15 to 20 minutes or until the squash is tender, stirring occasionally. Remove from heat. Spoon 1/3 of the squash mixture into a processor. Process until smooth. Repeat the process twice with the remaining squash mixture. Return the squash mixture to the saucepan. Stir in the half-and-half, salt and white pepper. Cook over low heat until heated through, stirring constantly. Ladle into soup bowls. Sprinkle with parsley and curry powder. May serve chilled.

Yield: 8 to 10 servings

Yogurt Flower

Drizzle a narrow circle of yogurt on the surface of soup. Add a dollop of yogurt in center. With a wooden pick, draw lines from the outer circle to center and back again until flower is complete.

Stuffed Fillet of Beef Tied with Leek Ribbons

1 (6-pound) beef fillet, trimmed
1 red bell pepper, julienned into
   2-inch pieces
1 leek, julienned into 2-inch
   pieces
2 carrots, julienned into
   2-inch pieces
2 cloves of garlic, minced
¼ cup unsalted butter
1 teaspoon chopped fresh
   rosemary or thyme
⅓ cup finely chopped parsley
Salt and freshly ground pepper
   to taste
Leek Ribbons (at left)
¼ cup melted butter

Make a lengthwise slit ³/4 way through fillet to form a pocket. Sauté bell pepper, leek, carrot and garlic in butter in a skillet just until tender. Stir in rosemary, parsley, salt and pepper. Stuff mixture into pocket; press sides together to enclose filling. Tie every 2 inches with kitchen twine. Place fillet in a roasting pan. Roast at 500 degrees for 15 minutes; remove from oven. Tie Leek Ribbons around fillet between the kitchen twine. Secure each knot and trim the edges. Brush fillet with melted butter. Roast for 7 minutes longer. Remove to serving platter. Discard kitchen twine. Slice between the leek "ribbons."

Yield: 12 servings

Leek Ribbons

Bring a saucepan of water to a boil. Separate the long leaves of the whole leek using a small sharp knife to slit the bottoms. Rinse to remove any dirt. Place the long leaves in the boiling water for 20 seconds. Remove quickly and plunge into ice water in a bowl; drain. Slice each leaf lengthwise into halves.

Blanched Asparagus with Hollandaise

8 ounces fresh asparagus per
   person
6 egg yolks
2 tablespoons lemon juice
⅛ teaspoon cayenne
1 cup butter

Snap off ends of asparagus by bending each stalk until tender portion is reached. Rinse well. Cook asparagus in a small amount of boiling water in a saucepan for 1 to 2 minutes for tiny spears, 3 to 5 minutes for small spears, 5 to 8 minutes for medium spears and 10 to 12 minutes for large spears; drain. Rinse with cold water or cover with ice. Combine egg yolks, lemon juice and cayenne in a processor. Process just until mixed. Heat butter in saucepan until bubbly. Add hot butter gradually to egg yolk mixture. Process for 30 seconds; let stand for 30 seconds. Repeat process until of desired consistency. Serve with asparagus.

Yield: Variable

Wild Mushroom Soufflé

1½ pounds mixed wild
    mushrooms, sliced
½ cup butter
¼ cup flour
3 egg yolks, lightly beaten
1 cup light cream
Salt and white pepper to taste
3 egg whites, stiffly beaten

Sauté the mushrooms in ¼ cup of the butter in a skillet until tender. Drain, reserving the juices. Heat the remaining ¼ cup butter in a saucepan until melted. Add the flour, whisking until blended. Stir in the egg yolks, light cream and reserved juices. Cook until thickened or of the desired sauce consistency, whisking constantly. Season with salt and white pepper. Remove from heat. Let stand until cool. Combine 1 cup of the sauce and the mushrooms in a bowl and mix gently. Fold in the egg whites. Spoon into a buttered 1½-quart baking dish. Place the baking dish in a larger baking pan filled with water to reach halfway up the sides of the baking dish. Bake at 350 degrees for 40 minutes.

Yield: 6 to 8 servings

Carrot Purée

1½ pounds carrots, peeled,
    cut into 2-inch slices
¼ cup butter
1 teaspoon sugar
⅛ teaspoon thyme
Salt and freshly ground pepper
    to taste
Nutmeg to taste

Combine the carrots with just enough water to cover in a saucepan. Add the butter and sugar. Cook over medium heat for 30 to 40 minutes or until very tender, stirring occasionally; drain. Process the carrots in a blender or food processor until smooth. Season with thyme, salt, pepper and nutmeg. Serve immediately.

Yield: 6 to 8 servings

Asparagus Accompaniments

Next time you cook asparagus, don't just think of Hollandaise sauce or lemon butter; use some of the following and cut your calories: chives, nutmeg, Parmesan cheese, parsley, poppy seed, sage, tarragon and thyme.

Cheese Herb Biscuits

2 cups flour
1 tablespoon baking powder
1 teaspoon salt
1/4 cup vegetable shortening
3/4 cup grated Gruyère cheese
1/4 cup chopped fresh dillweed
1 cup milk
2 tablespoons melted unsalted
    butter

Combine the flour, baking powder and salt in a processor bowl. Add shortening and process until it is the consistency of meal. Put in medium-size bowl. Stir in the cheese and dillweed. Add the milk, stirring until a soft dough forms that pulls away from the side of the bowl. Knead on a lightly floured surface just until the dough is mixed. Roll 1/2 inch thick; cut with a floured heart-shape cutter. Arrange on an ungreased baking sheet. Brush with the melted butter. Bake at 450 degrees for 12 to 15 minutes or until golden brown.

Yield: 12 to 14 biscuits

For a great appetizer, roast some garlic. Garlic is supposed to be very good for us physically, even if it tears us down socially.

Roasted Garlic Spread

1 giant head garlic

Remove the outer white papery skin of the garlic; do not separate the cloves. Wrap in foil. Bake at 350 degrees for 1 hour. Let stand for 10 minutes. Separate into cloves. Squeeze to extract the pulp, discarding the skins. Serve with toasted French bread slices or Cheese Herb Biscuits.

Yield: Variable

Coconut Crème Brûlée

Substitute 1 teaspoon vanilla extract if vanilla beans are not available.

1³/4 cups whipping cream

1³/4 cups milk

1 vanilla bean, split lengthwise
    into halves

6 egg yolks

1 egg

¹/2 cup sugar

²/3 cup packed flaked coconut,
    toasted, coarsely crumbled

¹/4 cup packed light brown
    sugar

Combine the whipping cream, milk and vanilla bean in a saucepan. Cook over medium-high heat just until the mixture comes to a boil. Remove from heat. Let stand for 10 minutes. Scrape the vanilla seeds into the milk mixture, reserving the pod for another use. Whisk the egg yolks, egg and sugar in a bowl until blended. Add the milk mixture gradually, whisking constantly. Skim off any froth. Spoon the coconut into eight ¹/2-cup ovenproof ramekins. Pour the custard mixture into the ramekins. Place the ramekins in a baking pan. Add hot water to reach halfway up the sides of the ramekins. Bake on the middle oven rack at 325 degrees for 40 minutes or until just set. Remove the ramekins to a wire rack to cool. Chill, covered loosely with plastic wrap, for 4 to 10 hours. Arrange the ramekins on a baking sheet. Sift the brown sugar over the custards. Broil 2 to 3 inches from the heat source for 2 minutes or until the sugar melts and caramelizes. If using raw sugar caramelize with a blowtorch. Chill for 20 minutes. Invert onto individual dessert plates.

Yield: 8 servings

An Elegant
Easter Luncheon

Menu

Orange Congealed Salad

Baked Ham with Brown Sugar Glaze

Pineapple Soufflé

Elegant Potatoes

Cold Asparagus with Sesame-Ginger Vinaigrette

Honey-Graham Sweet Potato Rolls

English Trifle

Minted Tea

*O*ur home, which is painted yellow brick trimmed in white, was named by our children years ago and the name "stuck"; thus Sunshine. There are plenty of windows to let the sunshine in, too. What a beautiful time of year to entertain your family and friends. The tulips and dogwoods are blooming, the forsythia adding its golden hue to the bunny scene. Now that we have seven grandchildren to entertain, an Easter egg hunt begins at 4 p.m. on Saturday of Easter weekend. Eggs are hidden before the children invade the scene, baskets are readied.

Last year a real bunny streaked across the yard just as the hunt began, as if the bunny was the master of the hunt just finishing the job of hiding the eggs—and signaling the start of the hunt. There are prizes for the most eggs and a picnic following. Dr. Bill takes the little ones for a "tractor trailer" ride all around the yard following the picnic.

Plan your egg hunt. Dye some of the eggs ahead and decorate. Buy individually wrapped candy and place in plastic eggs. We prepare 300 eggs for 30 children. There are prizes for the finder of the most eggs, the fewest eggs, and the golden egg. Everything is prepared as early as possible for the weekend as our entire family flocks in on Friday. There are seventeen of us now. The picnic is set up in the shady part of the yard by the gazebo. As a centerpiece on the picnic table, we use a yellow cloth and a basket lined with lettuce, radicchio, arugula, endive, etc. Tuck in a few hand-decorated or candy Easter eggs. Use decorative, heavy paper plates. Ice your drinks down in a wheelbarrow, wagon, or cooler. By all means use plastic cups. We generally have pimento cheese sandwiches, chicken salad sandwiches, pasta salad, fruit salad, and brownies.

At noon on Easter, after church, we enjoy lunch together. The table is set with the fine china on an antique linen cloth. Greenery and china eggs are combined for the centerpiece. With the crowd we have, a buffet works best. Every item in this menu may be prepared the day before your Easter luncheon. You may even prepare the Pineapple Soufflé and refrigerate unbaked. Remove soufflé from refrigerator two hours before serving and bake at the last minute.

Orange Congealed Salad

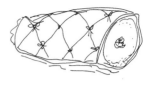

2 (6-ounce) packages orange
  gelatin
2 cups boiling water
1 cup orange juice
1 cup evaporated milk
1¹/₂ cups (5 to 6 medium) fresh
  orange sections or canned
  mandarin oranges
10 ounces frozen or dry flaked
  coconut

Dissolve the gelatin in boiling water in a
medium bowl. Stir in the orange juice. Chill
in the refrigerator for several minutes, stirring
occasionally; do not allow to begin congealing.
Blend in the evaporated milk. Chill the gelatin
mixture until the consistency of unbeaten egg
whites. Cut the orange sections into ¹/₂-inch
pieces. Stir the orange sections and coconut
into the partially congealed gelatin. Pour into
a 5-cup gelatin mold or a shallow 9x12-inch
dish. Chill for 3 hours or until firm. Unmold
the gelatin onto a serving platter. Garnish
with mint.

Yield: 8 to 10 servings

Baked Ham with Brown Sugar Glaze

*Ham is "hassle free" to fix. When serving ham, plan on four to
five servings per pound if the ham is boned, but count on only two to three
servings with a "bone-in" ham. Since the ham is fully cooked, you need
merely to heat it to serving temperature.*

1 (7- to 9-pound) smoked, fully
  cooked, whole boneless ham
Whole cloves
1 (8-ounce) bottle cola
³/₄ cup prepared mustard
3 cups packed dark brown
  sugar

Score the ham on the fat side in a diamond
design and place fat side up on a rack in a foil-
lined baking pan. Stud the ham with the cloves.
Pour the cola over the ham. Bake, uncovered,
at 325 degrees for 2 hours (18 to 24 minutes
per pound) or to 140 degrees on a meat
thermometer. Blend the mustard and brown
sugar in a small bowl. Spoon over the ham.
Bake for 10 minutes longer. Slice the ham
and serve.

Yield: 12 to 14 servings

Sage and Nuts

*Combine sage and curry
with stick cinnamon, star
anise, and an assortment
of nuts. Arrange on a
turkey or ham platter.*

Pineapple Soufflé

This is yummy and certainly complements the ham in this menu.

8 thick slices day-old bread,
  cut into cubes
2 cups drained crushed
  pineapple
4 eggs, beaten
1/2 cup melted unsalted butter
3/4 cup packed brown sugar

Combine the bread cubes and pineapple in a bowl and mix well. Pour into a greased 1 1/2-quart baking dish. Beat the eggs with the butter and brown sugar in a bowl and pour over the pineapple mixture. Bake at 350 degrees for 40 minutes or until puffed and golden brown. Serve immediately.

Yield: 6 to 8 servings

Elegant Potatoes

2 pounds small unpeeled red
  potatoes
1 cup sliced green onions
1/3 cup butter
2 cups sour cream
6 slices crisp-fried bacon,
  crumbled
2 cups shredded sharp
  Cheddar cheese
Salt and pepper to taste

Cook the potatoes in enough water to cover in a saucepan just until tender; drain. Let stand until cool. Slice the potatoes. Sauté the green onions in the butter in a skillet just until tender-crisp. Layer the potatoes, sour cream, green onions, bacon, Cheddar cheese, salt and pepper 1/2 at a time in a 3-quart baking dish sprayed with nonstick cooking spray. Bake at 350 degrees for 20 minutes. This is also delicious when made using reduced-fat sour cream and cheese.

Yield: 8 to 10 servings

Cold Asparagus with Sesame-Ginger Vinaigrette

A simple but elegant marriage of ginger, sesame and poached asparagus.

3 pounds fresh asparagus
    spears
Salt to taste
Sesame-Ginger Vinaigrette

Snap off the woody ends of the asparagus and rinse well. Bring lightly salted water to a boil in a medium skillet. Add the asparagus spears and cook for 5 minutes or just until tender-crisp. Drain and plunge the asparagus into ice water to stop the cooking process. Pat the asparagus dry and arrange on a serving platter. Drizzle the desired amount of Sesame-Ginger Vinaigrette evenly over the asparagus. Serve immediately.

Yield: 10 servings

Sesame-Ginger Vinaigrette

3 tablespoons sesame seeds
3 small cloves of garlic
1 tablespoon grated fresh
    gingerroot
1/4 cup rice vinegar
1/4 cup orange juice
4 teaspoons soy sauce
3 tablespoons vegetable oil
3 tablespoons sugar
3/4 teaspoon red chile flakes
1/2 cup sesame oil

Toast the sesame seeds by placing in a small skillet and heating over medium heat until fragrant and just golden in color, stirring frequently. Watch carefully. Combine the toasted sesame seeds, garlic, ginger, vinegar, orange juice, soy sauce, vegetable oil, sugar, chile flakes and sesame oil in a blender and process until thoroughly combined.

Asparagus

Asparagus is my favorite vegetable. When blanching, do not overcook. Drain quickly and place ice over hot asparagus to cool it quickly. This stops the cooking process and the asparagus will keep its nice fresh color. For a fun spring project, plant an asparagus bed. Locate it on slanting part of yard or garden so that it will drain well. Use a sandy soil and manure for fertilizer. Cut back and mulch just before frost. It is so exciting to see the first stalks peeping up in the early spring. It takes three years to have a well-established bed.

Honey-Graham Sweet Potato Rolls

1 cup all-purpose flour
1¹/2 cups whole wheat flour
³/4 teaspoon salt
1 envelope quick-rising yeast
¹/2 cup mashed cooked sweet
  potatoes
¹/3 cup honey
2 tablespoons vegetable oil
1 egg white
¹/3 cup syrup from canned
  sweet potatoes, or water
¹/3 cup melted butter or
  margarine
2 tablespoons honey
1¹/2 cups graham cracker
  crumbs

Combine the flours, salt and yeast in a food processor fitted with the metal blade and pulse to mix well. Add the sweet potatoes, ¹/3 cup honey, oil and egg white and process until blended. Heat the sweet potato syrup until warm to the touch. Add just enough of the warm liquid to the processor until the mixture forms a ball, processing constantly. Process for 1 minute longer to knead; the dough should be sticky. Knead the dough lightly on a lightly floured surface. Shape into a ball. Place in a greased bowl, turning to coat the surface. Let rise, covered with a damp towel, in a warm place until doubled in bulk. Punch the dough down and turn onto a lightly floured surface. Knead a few times and divide into 12 portions. Shape each portion into a ball. Blend the butter and 2 tablespoons honey in a small bowl. Place the crumbs in a plastic bag. Roll each dough ball in the honey mixture and shake in the crumbs to coat. Arrange the coated balls in a greased 9-inch round baking pan, placing close together. Let rest for 10 minutes. Bake at 400 degrees for 25 to 30 minutes or until golden brown. Recipe may be doubled.

Yield: 12 large rolls

English Trifle

1 (8-inch) yellow or white cake
  layer
1 (8-ounce) jar raspberry
  preserves
¹/4 to ¹/2 cup sherry
Custard
1 cup whipping cream
3 tablespoons confectioners'
  sugar
¹/2 cup toasted sliced almonds

Split the cake into 2 layers. Spread the
preserves between the layers. Cut the cake into
12 slices. Arrange half the slices in a 2- to 3-
quart trifle bowl. Sprinkle with half the sherry.
Spoon half the Custard over the cake slices.
Repeat the layers with the remaining cake,
sherry and Custard. Whip the cream with the
confectioners' sugar until peaks form. Spread
over the Custard and sprinkle with the almonds.
Chill for 4 hours or longer before serving.
May substitute fresh strawberries, blueberries
or peaches or a combination of the three for
the preserves.

Yield: 12 servings

Custard

¹/2 cup sugar
¹/2 teaspoon salt
2 tablespoons cornstarch
2¹/2 cups milk
4 egg yolks, beaten
2 teaspoons vanilla extract

Combine sugar, salt and cornstarch in a
1¹/2-quart microwave-safe bowl and mix well.
Stir in milk gradually. Microwave on High for
7 minutes or until slightly thickened. Stir a
little more than half of the hot mixture into egg
yolks and stir the egg yolk mixture into the hot
mixture, blending well. Microwave on Medium-
High for 5 to 6 minutes longer, stirring after 2
minutes. Let the custard stand until cool. Stir
in the vanilla.

Minted Tea

2 family-size tea bags
1 cup sugar
³/4 cup packed fresh mint
  leaves
Juice of 2 lemons
1 quart boiling water
1 quart cold water
Fresh mint sprigs

Combine the tea bags,
sugar, mint leaves and
lemon juice in a 2-quart
Pyrex cup or pitcher.
Add the boiling water
and steep, covered, for
5 to 10 minutes. Strain
the mixture into a pitcher
and discard the tea bags
and mint leaves. Add the
cold water. Serve over
crushed ice and garnish
with mint sprigs.

Yield: 2 quarts

A Holiday
Appetizer Buffet

Menu

Baked Fiesta Spinach Dip

Cheese Fondue with Fresh Vegetables

Brie with Bourbon Praline Topping with Bremner Wafers

West Indies Salad

Vegetable Frittata

Sun-Dried Tomato and Gruyère Cheese Puffs

Black-Eyed Pea Relish with Bagel Chips

Sliced Smoked Turkey, Ham, and Barbecue on Dill Bread with Mustard Sauce

Chocolate-Orange Truffles

Plum Pudding with Hard Sauce • Holiday Punch

The cocktail or appetizer party is a peculiarly American institution. It has developed in this country, with guests standing and moving around, and it perfectly suits our love of mobility, informality and "snacking." This party is a kind of dinner substitute. It's a great way to entertain a lot of people.

Even the most experienced hosts organize the tasks of preparing for a party. Make a game plan, shop smart, and serve with pizzazz.

Remember to send your invitations a month early since so much is happening during the holidays. The dill bread, baked spinach dip, vegetable frittata, and chocolate truffles can be done a couple of weeks ahead and kept frozen. Be sure your countdown lists and grocery list are made early. Two days ahead, prepare all the sauces, make cheese puffs, buy all the groceries, cut up the vegetables and store in ziplock bags, and make Black-Eyed Pea Relish. The day before your party, thaw out appetizers and truffles in refrigerator and cut frittata in squares; make West Indies Salad and cheese fondue. Be sure you have enough crackers and bagel chips. Check all your serving pieces, set your buffet table layout. Many people are putting food all over the house—coffee tables, dining room, and breakfast room—to spread out the crowd.

The day of the party, cover your Brie with praline glaze—place on something that you can run into the microwave to soften it, just before serving. Then transfer to the platter. Arrange all of your platters and trays and garnish them. I usually use flowers, bows, ribbons, and herbs to garnish.

We always serve plum pudding provided by Warrington Plum Pudding Company (see page 90) at our parties during the holidays. The pudding now comes with directions for steaming in the microwave. After steaming the pudding, cut in tiny pieces, place in gold or silver foil cups, and top with a teaspoon of hard sauce.

Baked Fiesta Spinach Dip

1 cup chopped onion
1 tablespoon vegetable oil
1 cup chunky medium salsa,
   well drained
1 (10-ounce) package frozen
   chopped spinach, thawed
2¹/2 cups shredded Monterey
   Jack cheese
8 ounces light cream cheese,
   cubed
1 cup light cream
¹/2 cup sliced black olives
1 cup chopped pecans

Sauté the onion in oil in a medium skillet over medium heat until tender. Add the salsa. Drain the spinach and squeeze dry. Add the spinach to the skillet. Cook for 2 minutes. Pour the mixture into 1¹/2-quart baking dish. Stir in 2 cups of the Monterey Jack and the cream cheese, cream and olives. Sprinkle with the pecans. Bake, uncovered, at 350 degrees for 15 minutes. Cover with foil and bake for 15 minutes longer. Sprinkle with the remaining ¹/2 cup Monterey Jack. Serve hot.

Yield: 5 cups

Cheese Fondue

1 clove of garlic
1¹/2 cups Chablis or other dry
   white wine
8 cups (2 pounds) shredded
   Swiss cheese
¹/4 cup all-purpose flour
¹/2 teaspoon salt
¹/2 teaspoon dry mustard
¹/8 teaspoon ground nutmeg
2 tablespoons cognac or
   light rum

Cut the garlic clove into halves and rub the bottom and side of large saucepan with the garlic. Discard the garlic. Pour the wine into the prepared saucepan. Heat the wine over medium heat but do not allow to boil. Combine the cheese and flour in a large bowl and toss until the cheese is lightly coated with the flour. Add the cheese to the hot wine gradually. Heat until the cheese melts, stirring constantly. Stir in the salt, dry mustard, nutmeg and cognac. Pour the fondue into a fondue pot or chafing dish to keep warm. Serve with bread cubes, apple slices or bite-size fresh vegetables for dipping.

Yield: 5 cups

Give the gift of hospitality in your home this season. Bedeck the entire household with touches of holiday fun, and prepare to entertain friends and family like it's never been done before. 'Tis the season to make your own magic. The buffet table is set, the fire is crackling, and the tree is glistening. Set the mood with music. The fabric of the holidays is woven with family, friends, fabulous food, favorite gifts, and seasonal decorating touches.

Brie with Bourbon Praline Topping

1 cup (8 ounces) melted butter
3 cups packed dark brown
   sugar
1¹/2 cups pecans
¹/3 cup bourbon
1 (5-pound) Brie

Combine the butter and brown sugar in a bowl
and mix well. Stir in the pecans and bourbon.
Place the Brie on a large platter. Spread the
pecan mixture over the Brie. Microwave the
Brie on High for 1 minute just before serving.
May order whole round of Brie through your
deli department.

Yield: 40 to 50 appetizers

West Indies Salad

*For your buffet centerpiece,
fill a tall hurricane lamp
with fruits like apples,
pears, or cranberries. Top
it off with fresh green
holly, and holly and
evergreen at the base, with
votive candles scattered
among the greenery.*

1 medium onion, finely
   chopped
1 pound fresh crab meat
¹/2 cup vegetable oil
¹/2 cup ice water
5 tablespoons cider vinegar
1 tablespoon fresh lemon juice
Salt and freshly ground pepper
   to taste

Layer half the onion, crab meat and remaining
onion in a large bowl. Combine the vegetable
oil, ice water, vinegar, lemon juice, salt and
pepper in a small bowl and mix well. Pour over
the onion and crab meat layers. Refrigerate,
tightly covered, for 2 to 12 hours. Toss the
mixture before serving. Serve with Bremner
wafers. Doubles easily.

Yield: 12 to 14 servings

Vegetable Frittata

1 large Spanish onion

3 cloves of garlic

3 medium summer squash

3 medium zucchini

1 red bell pepper

1 yellow bell pepper

1 green bell pepper

8 ounces fresh mushrooms

3 tablespoons olive oil

6 eggs

$1/4$ cup heavy or whipping cream

2 teaspoons salt

2 teaspoons freshly ground pepper

2 cups ($1/2$-inch) dried French bread cubes

8 ounces cream cheese, finely chopped

2 cups shredded Swiss cheese

Thinly slice the onion and mince the garlic. Cut the squash and zucchini into $1/4$-inch slices. Seed the bell peppers and cut into $1/4$-inch strips. Slice the mushrooms. Heat the olive oil in a large saucepan over medium-high heat. Add the vegetables. Sauté the vegetables for 15 to 20 minutes or until tender-crisp. Whisk the eggs and cream in a large bowl. Add the salt and pepper. Add the bread cubes, cream cheese and Swiss cheese and mix well. Add the sautéed vegetables and mix well. Pour into a greased 10-inch springform pan or a 9x13-inch baking pan, packing the mixture firmly. Place the pan on a baking sheet. Bake at 350 degrees for about 1 hour or until firm to the touch, puffed and golden brown. Cover the top with foil to prevent overbrowning if necessary. Place the springform pan on a serving plate, loosen the frittata from the side and remove the side of the pan. Cut into small squares. Serve the frittata hot, at room temperature or cold. May reheat cooled frittata at 350 degrees for 15 minutes or until warmed through if desired.

Yield: 48 small appetizers

Some of the wines at our parties are furnished by St. James Winery, St. James, Missouri. St. James Winery is the Hofherr family-owned business of our daughter and son-in-law, Peter, and Sheri Hofherr, the Hofherr brothers, and mother, Pat Hofherr. They have won Bon-Appetit, state, and national awards, with their wines.

A Holiday Appetizer Buffet

Mustard and Jalapeño Dressing

¹/₂ cup olive oil
3 tablespoons red wine
   vinegar
1 to 2 tablespoons whole-
   grain mustard
1 fresh jalapeño, seeded,
   minced
Salt and freshly ground
   pepper to taste

Combine olive oil, red wine
vinegar, mustard, jalapeño,
salt and pepper in a small
bowl and whisk until
well mixed.

Sun-Dried Tomato and Gruyère Cheese Puffs

1 cup water
¹/₂ cup unsalted butter
¹/₈ teaspoon salt
1 cup sifted all-purpose flour
4 eggs
4 ounces Gruyère cheese,
   shredded
2 ounces sun-dried tomatoes,
   minced

Combine the water, butter and salt in a
saucepan and bring to a boil. Add the flour all
at once and mix well. Cook until smooth,
stirring constantly. Remove from heat and place
the mixture in a food processor container. Add
the eggs 1 at a time, processing until smooth
after each addition. Add the cheese and sun-
dried tomatoes and stir until mixed. Drop by
tablespoonfuls onto an ungreased baking sheet.
Bake at 425 degrees for 10 minutes. Reduce
the oven temperature to 350 degrees. Bake for
5 to 10 minutes longer or until golden brown.
Remove to a wire rack to cool. Cut into halves
and fill with egg salad, Boursin cheese or
marinated goat cheese.

Yield: 24 puffs

Black-Eyed Pea Relish

2 (15-ounce) cans black-eyed
   peas
2 scallions
1 red bell pepper
¹/₂ green bell pepper (optional)
¹/₄ cup chopped fresh flat
   Italian parsley
¹/₄ cup finely chopped fresh
   chervil (optional)
1 clove of garlic, minced
Mustard and Jalapeño Dressing
   (at left)

Drain the peas, rinse and drain well. Cut the
scallions into ¹/₂-inch pieces. Seed the bell
peppers and chop finely. Combine the peas,
scallions, bell peppers, parsley, chervil and garlic
in large salad bowl. Add the Mustard and
Jalapeño Dressing and toss to mix. Serve
immediately with bagel chips.

Yield: 12 to 14 servings

Dill Bread

What a wonderful accompaniment to any meat for a cocktail supper. This is one of my favorite recipes. It goes great with pimento cheese, too.

1 envelope dry yeast
¹/₄ cup warm (105- to
   115-degree) water
1 cup cream-style cottage cheese
1 egg, slightly beaten
2 tablespoons sugar
1 tablespoon minced onion
1 tablespoon butter or
   margarine, softened
2 teaspoons dillseeds
2¹/₂ cups all-purpose flour
1 teaspoon salt
¹/₄ teaspoon baking soda
1 to 2 tablespoons melted
   butter
Salt to taste

Dissolve the yeast in warm water in a large warm bowl. Heat the cottage cheese in a saucepan to lukewarm. Add to yeast and mix well. Add the egg, sugar, onion, 1 tablespoon butter and dillseeds and mix well. Sift the flour with 1 teaspoon salt and baking soda and add to the cottage cheese mixture. Stir until well blended; the dough will be quite soft. Let the dough rise, loosely covered, for about 1 hour. Spoon the dough into 2 greased 3x8-inch loaf pans. Let rise, loosely covered, for 1 hour. Bake at 350 degrees for 30 to 35 minutes or until golden brown. Brush the loaves with melted butter and sprinkle with salt to taste. Invert onto wire racks to cool. Chill before slicing.

Yield: 2 loaves

Mustard Sauce

May serve with oven-roasted Barbecued Brisket (page 57). Generally, someone gives us a turkey and a ham which we add to our Holiday Appetizer Buffet.

1 cup dry mustard
   (preferably Colemans)
1 cup white vinegar
2 eggs
1 cup sugar
¹/₂ teaspoon salt

Place the dry mustard in a small saucepan. Whisk the vinegar into the mustard gradually until smooth. Beat the eggs well and stir eggs, sugar and salt into the mustard mixture. Cook over medium heat until thickened, stirring constantly. Let stand until cool. Store in a tightly covered jar in the refrigerator.

Yield: 2 cups

Tussy Mussy

Tie clusters of oregano, rosemary, sage, and thyme with ribbon or braid for a fragrant nosegay. Add small rosebuds to the bunch if desired. Use on any food tray.

Plum Pudding

We always enjoy Plum Pudding and rum cakes over the holidays. Our son and daughter-in-law, along with Alice and Bruce Brewer, Tara's parents, own Warrington Plum Pudding Company in Nashville, Tennessee. The company just celebrated its 50th anniversary. Mrs. Nancy De Luca started the company in 1945 to support her family when her husband died. Tara and Bill bought the company in 1991. It is a mail order company specializing in plum pudding, rum cakes, and fruit cakes. To order or for information, call 1-800-232-3694.

Chocolate Orange Truffles

¹/₄ cup butter
¹/₃ cup whipping cream
7 ounces semisweet chocolate
1 egg yolk
1 teaspoon grated orange peel
2 tablespoons Grand Marnier (optional)
Unsweetened cocoa powder or finely chopped pecans

Cut the butter into small pieces and combine with the whipping cream in a small saucepan. Cook over low heat until the butter melts and the cream bubbles around the edge. Remove from the heat. Cut the chocolate into small pieces and add to the hot cream mixture. Let stand, covered, for several minutes or until the chocolate melts. Stir until the mixture is smooth. Add the egg yolk and stir until smooth. Add the orange peel and Grand Marnier and mix well. Chill the mixture until firm. Shape into 1-inch balls and roll in cocoa powder or pecans to coat. Store in the refrigerator. To serve, place in miniature silver or gold foil candy cups. May prepare by microwaving the butter, whipping cream and chocolate in a microwave-safe dish until blended, stirring occasionally, if preferred. Stir until the mixture is smooth. Stir a small amount of the hot mixture into the egg yolk; stir the egg yolk into the hot mixture. Mix in the orange peel and Grand Marnier. Proceed accordingly.

Yield: 20 servings

Holiday Punch

4 cups cranberry juice

1¹/2 cups sugar

4 cups pineapple juice

1 tablespoon almond extract
  (optional)

Holiday Ice Mold
  or pineapple juice ice
  cubes

2 quarts ginger ale, chilled

Combine the cranberry juice, sugar, pineapple juice and almond extract in a 1-gallon container and mix until the sugar dissolves. Chill the mixture until serving time. Place the mixture in a punch bowl. Add the Holiday Ice Mold or pineapple juice ice cubes. Add the ginger ale just before serving. Garnish with holly sprigs.

Yield: 25 (5-ounce) servings

Holiday Ice Mold

Fill a 6-cup ring mold half full with water. Freeze until firm. Arrange your choice of leaves and/or fruit decoratively on the frozen layer. Add a small amount of water to secure the fruit and leaves in place. Freeze until firm. Add water to fill the mold and return to the freezer overnight or up to 1 week. Unmold by dipping the bottom of the mold in cold water to loosen and inverting onto heavy-duty foil. Wrap the mold tightly in foil and store in the freezer until needed. Unwrap the mold and place in the punch bowl, decorative side up.

Frosted Fruit

This is fabulous as a holiday centerpiece, placed on a crystal or silver cake pedestal with ribbons added in swirls on top and extended down the table.

1 egg white

Fruit of choice such as grapes,
  plums, crab apples, pears
  and apples

Sugar

Whip the egg white with a fork until frothy. Rinse the fruit and pat dry. Brush the egg white over the surface of the fruit and sift sugar over the fruit to coat. Place the fruit on a wire rack; do not allow pieces to touch. Let stand until dry.

Yield: Variable

A Southern
Wedding Reception

Menu

Curried Cheese Ball • Cheese Straws (page 19)

Almond Brandy Mold with Bremner Wafers

Fontina Tomato Squares

Belgian Endive with Roquefort Cheese

Fresh Fruit Cascading Out of Baskets with Lemon Mousse

Hot Shrimp and Artichokes with Toast Points

Pork Tenderloin on Herbed Polenta with Red Onion Marmalade

Asparagus in the Pink

Lemon Mousse Wedding Cake

Groom's Cake • Champagne Punch

The formal wedding and reception is making a comeback. No longer are weddings the homespun affairs they once were. Even if the couple vows theirs will be a "small" wedding, before it is over things and lists have blossomed, and simplicity doesn't stand a chance. Our wedding menu should assist you in selecting foods to serve at your weddings, since they are generally held at clubs, hotels, etc.

If the tent doesn't blow away and the electricity doesn't go off, then the tables of food sinking into the ground surely will add an air of excitement to the event. All of these things did happen at our daughter Lisa's wedding. The happy caterer, mother of the bride, me, and the always prepared father, Doc Bill, were expecting a rather large group of 500 in a tent in the back yard for the reception. The rain had been relentless and the ground was soggy. Bill had thought ahead in the week before and dug the trenches around the tent, with sump pumps "in case" there was more rain. As you might know, the day of the wedding there were clear skies in the morning, the tent was gorgeous, decorated by the talented Carl Cassidy of Sheffield, Alabama, and the food in the final stages at Johnston Street Cafe. All looked perfect on the home front. Storm clouds were gathering, however.

After the wedding, as we entered the tent filled with happy people, the wind began to blow. Someone rushed in to tell us a tornado was headed our way from Cullman, and that we should clear the tent. The rain began in great torrents. I shouted, "Everyone should take cover and get into the house." Not many people moved an inch or a muscle as everyone was having too much fun. All of a sudden, the electricity went out in the house and the tent. The band, of course, was no longer able to play, and we were in virtual darkness, with the wind "doing a number" and the lightening flashing. My sister, Catherine, located boxes of candles in the house that Bill had bought weeks ago at Sandlin's "Going out of Business Sale," so she dispersed them everywhere with willing guests helping.

Well, the tent did not blow away, no one was injured, and the reception went on. The wind subsided finally, the tornado passed us by, and Decaturites and wedding reception attendees from out of town are still talking about the candle lit reception, complete with totally ruined shoes for everyone, and the bride's dress covered in mud. The house is still standing and we occasionally find candle tallow in funny places. All reported a wonderful and interestingly fun time.

If you do decide to "cater" your own daughter's wedding reception, it is possible. Decide on a simple menu at an hour when the guests would not be ravenous. Otherwise hire a caterer.

If you do choose to cater the reception, you must first find or determine a location, time, number attending, etc. A simple menu for the occasion would be punch, cheese straws, finger sandwiches, fresh fruit and dip, and wedding cake. This is gracious plenty, just have a lot of each since you are offering only a few items. One gallon of punch will serve 32 people one 4-ounce cup; I would allow each guest two 4-ounce cups. Plan for each guest to have 3 cheese straws, 3 finger sandwiches, 3 pieces of fruit, and 1 piece of cake. By all means, decorate with Jackson vine as my daughter, Sheri, says that no Southern function is ever without Jackson vine. If you do not want to go to the expense of flowers it is perfectly appropriate to use just greenery in the church as well as the reception area. If an evening wedding, candles add the welcomed glow.

Curried Cheese Ball

2¼ pounds sharp Cheddar
   cheese, shredded
24 ounces cream cheese,
   softened
1 jar Major Grey chutney
1 tablespoon curry powder
1½ teaspoons dry mustard
1 cup chopped pecans, toasted

Process the Cheddar cheese and cream cheese in a food processor until smooth. Add the chutney, curry powder and dry mustard. Process until blended. Shape into a ball. Roll in the pecans. Garnish with additional chutney. Serve with thin wheat or rye crackers.

Yield: 50 servings

Almond Brandy Mold

*This is one of my favorite recipes. Everyone always asks for the recipe.
I took this to a Derby Party once and people almost forgot the race because
they were busy eating this appetizer.*

1 cup slivered almonds
1 cup golden raisins
Grated peel of 2 lemons
½ cup brandy
1 envelope unflavored gelatin
¼ cup cold water
12 ounces cream cheese,
   softened
½ cup butter, softened
½ cup sour cream
½ cup sugar

Combine the almonds, raisins and lemon peel in a bowl and mix well. Add brandy to cover and mix well. Let stand for 8 to 10 hours; drain. Combine the gelatin and cold water in a small bowl and mix well. Let stand for 5 minutes to soften. Place over hot water, stirring until dissolved. Process the cream cheese, butter, sour cream and sugar in a food processor until smooth. Add the gelatin mixture. Process until blended. Stir in the almonds, raisins and lemon peel. Spoon into a greased 1-quart mold. Chill until set. Invert onto a serving platter. Serve with wheat biscuits or Bremner wafers.

Yield: 35 servings

Wedding Reception Tips

- Wedding receptions are becoming a bit more casual in many cases. People are doing things that they did not do five years ago—anything goes.

- Decide on size, style and budget.

- Set the date—book caterer (if using), florist, church, and reception hall, of course, and photographer.

Wedding Reception Tips

- Seek out good resources and get recommendations.

- Have a written agreement or contract with all vendors.

- Devise a master "to do" list for vendors, gift registration, and wedding party.

- Trust your own judgement and relax—let helpers you have carefully selected take over.

Fontina Tomato Squares

1 cup unsalted butter, softened
8 ounces cream cheese, softened
1 teaspoon salt
1 teaspoon thyme
2 cups unbleached flour
3 tablespoons Dijon mustard
5 ripe medium tomatoes, thinly sliced
3 cups (6-ounces) coarsely grated Italian fontina cheese
3 tablespoons finely shredded fresh basil
2 tablespoons olive oil
Kosher salt and freshly ground pepper to taste

Process butter, cream cheese, salt and thyme in a food processor until blended. Add flour. Process until dough forms a ball. Pat dough into a rectangle; wrap in waxed paper. Chill for 1 hour. Pat dough 1/4 inch thick on a lightly floured surface. Cut into a 14x18-inch rectangle. Pat dough over bottom and up sides of a 12x16-inch baking pan. Bake at 375 degrees for 20 to 25 minutes or until golden brown. Poke any bubbles which form on the pastry during baking process with tip of a sharp knife. Cool slightly. Brush baked layer with Dijon mustard. Arrange tomatoes in a single layer over mustard. Sprinkle with fontina cheese and basil. Drizzle with olive oil. Sprinkle with salt and pepper. Bake for 20 minutes or until bubbly. Cut into squares. Serve warm or at room temperature. May substitute Swiss cheese for the fontina cheese.

Yield: 40 servings

Belgian Endive with Roquefort Cheese

3 ounces (6 tablespoons) cream cheese, softened
2 ounces (1/4 cup) Roquefort cheese, softened
1 tablespoon brandy
1 1/2 teaspoons lemon juice
1/8 teaspoon cayenne
4 heads endive, separated into 30 to 36 spears
Chopped fresh parsley

Combine the cream cheese, Roquefort cheese, brandy, lemon juice and cayenne in a food processor container. Process until blended. Chill, covered, in the refrigerator. Pipe or spoon 1 teaspoon of the cheese mixture onto the stem end of each endive spear. Sprinkle lightly with parsley.

Yield: 30 to 36 servings

Hot Shrimp and Artichokes

This recipe may be doubled or tripled for larger crowds.

2 pounds mushrooms
3 cups butter
4 cups flour
16 cups milk
1 cup sherry
2 tablespoons Worcestershire
    sauce
Salt and pepper to taste
4 cups grated Parmesan cheese
4 pounds shrimp, cooked,
    peeled, deveined
8 (16-ounce) cans artichoke
    hearts, drained, chopped
Toast Points

Sauté the mushrooms in 1 cup of the butter in a saucepan until tender. Heat the remaining 2 cups butter in a large saucepan until melted. Add the flour, whisking until blended. Whisk in the milk. Cook until thickened, stirring constantly. Stir in the sherry, Worcestershire sauce, salt, pepper and cheese. Add the shrimp, artichokes and mushrooms. Spoon into a chafing dish. Serve with Toast Points. May be prepared 1 day in advance or early in the day and stored in the refrigerator until just before serving. Reheat in the microwave or on the stove just until heated through. Add the shrimp just before the final heating.

Yield: 35 servings

Toast Points

White bread slices, crusts
    trimmed

Cut each bread slice into 4 triangles. Arrange on a baking sheet. Bake at 300 degrees for 30 minutes; do not brown. Prepare 2 toast points per guest.

Wedding Reception Tips

• Reconfirm all details one to two weeks in advance.

• Be realistic about calculating expenses— your reception will be the most expensive item, so that will give you the most opportunity to save on flowers and food. It is not necessary to have a great deal of food. Schedule wedding at an hour where only light fare is expected.

Pork Tenderloin

3 pounds pork tenderloin
Honey cup mustard or sweet
  mustard
Salt and pepper to taste

Rinse the pork tenderloin and pat dry. Arrange in a baking pan. Sprinkle lightly with salt and pepper. Bake at 325 degrees for 30 minutes. Spread the honey cup mustard over the tenderloin. Bake for 30 minutes longer or until a meat thermometer registers 170 degrees.

Yield: 30 servings

Herbed Polenta

5¹/₂ cups water
1¹/₂ cups yellow cornmeal or
  polenta meal
¹/₂ teaspoon salt
1 tablespoon minced fresh
  herbs (rosemary, thyme,
  chives, parsley)
2 tablespoons chopped green
  onions

Whisk the water, cornmeal and salt together in a 3-quart microwave-safe bowl. Microwave, covered, on High for 9 minutes, beating every 3 minutes until smooth; remove cover. Stir in fresh herbs and green onions. Microwave on High for 4 minutes and beat. Microwave for 4 minutes longer and beat. Spread in a 9x13-inch dish. Let stand until room temperature. Cut into desired shapes. Reheat in the microwave, grill or sauté in oil until light brown. Serve immediately. May be prepared in advance, stored in the refrigerator and reheated just before serving. Omit the fresh herbs and green onions to prepare Basic Polenta.

Yield: Variable

Red Onion Marmalade

2 large red onions, thinly sliced
3 tablespoons brown sugar
3/4 cup dry red wine
3 tablespoons balsamic vinegar
Salt and pepper to taste

Combine the onions and brown sugar in a saucepan. Cook over medium heat for 20 to 25 minutes or until the onions begin to caramelize and turn golden brown, stirring frequently. Stir in the red wine and balsamic vinegar. Bring to a boil over medium-high heat; reduce heat. Cook over low heat for 15 minutes or until most of the liquid has been absorbed, stirring frequently. Season with salt and pepper. Chill, covered, in the refrigerator for up to 3 weeks. Serve at room temperature.

Yield: 1 cup

Asparagus in the Pink

3 pounds fresh asparagus
Pink Sauce (at right)

Select bright green asparagus spears. Discard the pithy tough stalks and rinse. Combine the asparagus with a small amount of boiling water in a saucepan. Bring to a boil. Boil for 7 minutes. If asparagus is pencil thin, boil slightly less. Drain in a colander; cover with ice. Let stand until cool. Drain on paper towels. Serve with Pink Sauce. Serve the asparagus within 3 hours or chill, covered, in single layers separated by paper towels in a storage container.

Yield: 30 servings

Pink Sauce

3 cups mayonnaise
2 (4-ounce) jars roasted
    pimento peppers
1/2 teaspoon cayenne

Combine the mayonnaise, pimento peppers and cayenne in a food processor container. Process for 1 minute.

Yield: 4 cups

Lemon Mousse Wedding Cake

24 eggs, at room temperature
3 cups sugar
6 cups cake flour, sifted
1 cup poppy seeds (optional)
9 tablespoons grated lemon
  peel
$^1/_2$ cup melted butter
Lemon Mousse (page 101)
Swiss Meringue Buttercream
  Frosting

Butter and flour two 6-inch cake pans, two 10-inch cake pans and two 14-inch cake pans. Line with parchment paper. Beat the eggs in a mixer bowl until light and creamy; volume should be about 4 times the original. Add the sugar and mix well. Fold in a mixture of the cake flour and poppy seeds. Stir in the lemon peel and butter. Fill cake pans 3/4 full. Bake at 350 degrees for 30 minutes or until wooden pick inserted in the center comes out clean. Cool in the pans on wire racks. Invert onto a cake plate. Spread Lemon Mousse between the layers. Spread Swiss Meringue Buttercream over the top and sides of the cake. Store, covered, in the refrigerator.

Yield: 150 servings

Swiss Meringue Buttercream Frosting

4 cups (approximately 30)
  egg whites
8 cups sugar
5 pounds unsalted butter
2 pounds white chocolate,
  melted, cooled slightly

Combine the egg whites and sugar in a large mixer bowl. Place over simmering water. Simmer until the mixture is warm and the sugar has dissolved, whisking occasionally. Remove from heat. Beat at high speed until stiff peaks form. Beat at medium speed until the meringue reaches room temperature. Add the butter gradually, beating constantly at medium speed until blended. Beat at high speed for 1 to 2 minutes. Add the white chocolate. Beat at medium speed until smooth and of spreading consistency. Store, covered, in the refrigerator for up to 3 weeks. Beat for several minutes before using to return to spreading consistency. Do not substitute slightly salted butter for unsalted butter.

Lemon Mousse

This is excellent as a dip with fresh fruit.

1/2 cup unsalted butter
1 1/2 cups sugar
4 eggs, beaten
Juice of 3 lemons
1 1/2 teaspoons grated lemon
    peel
2 cups whipping cream,
    whipped

Melt the butter in a 2-quart Pyrex cup. Add the sugar, eggs, lemon juice and lemon peel; blend well. Microwave on High for 4 minutes; whisk. Microwave on Medium-High for 4 minutes; whisk. Microwave for 4 minutes longer; whisk. Let stand until cool. Fold in the whipped cream. Serve with assorted fresh fruit.

Yield: 5 cups

Champagne Punch

Very easy and delicious. Mix everything in advance except the Champagne, or have all of the ingredients chilled and merely pour them over a fruit ice ring or block of ice in a punch bowl.

2 quarts Champagne, chilled
2 quarts apple juice, chilled
2 fifths light rum, chilled
2 tablespoons Angostura bitters,
    chilled
Holiday Ice Mold (page 91)

Combine the Champagne, apple juice, rum and bitters in a large container. Pour over an ice ring in a punch bowl. Ladle into punch cups.

Yield: 50 servings

Tulips

Multicolored tulip petals offer endless possibilities for a garnish. They can be stuffed with dip or shrimp salad once the pollen and stigma have been removed.

Johnston Street Cafe Favorites

Contents

*L*ong a dream, at last a reality. Johnston Street Cafe was born and very much alive on February 8, 1988. After many years of observing and planning and with the expert advice of my friend Bonny Bailey in Birmingham, we progressed with a plan. Bonnie had allowed me to work with her at her restaurant, The Highland Gourmet, to be sure that this was what I really wanted to get into. Ann Pollard, my friend who now owns the Green Bottle Restaurant in Huntsville, was my constant companion in planning Johnston Street Cafe, and helped me execute the final plan. We opened with a bang and lines out the door for weeks. Martha Orr and India Harris were my first management team. Sally Smartt and Carolyn Tweedy were my darling cheerleaders, encouraging me all the way to "go ahead with my dream." My family could not have been more supportive. My husband, Bill, with his usual enthusiasm was a constant source of inspiration. Located in a very historic building built in the 19th century, it required much renovation. Libby Sims Patrick, our daughter, who is an interior designer, was responsible for planning and designing the interior space. Since there was a very low ceiling (we could hardly stand up without hitting our heads in the dining area) we excavated three feet of dirt to get more height, and Libby designed a special ceiling to give the effect of height. We came up with an efficient design and painted the entire shop a lovely peach with white trim. Johnston Street Cafe is open from 8:00 a.m. until 5:30 p.m. Muffins, sweet rolls and fresh fruit can be enjoyed early morning. Lunch is served at noon with many deli salads, sandwiches, soups, and a hot entrée of the day plus "scrumptious" desserts. There is a great business of pick-up entrées, salads, breads, and desserts from the take-out freezer and cooler late in the afternoon. Normally, things ran very smoothly at Johnston Street while I was owner, with the able help of Joan Holland. We do a lot of catering, quite a bit of it for weddings. There was one day that I do consider my "Catering Day From Hell." We had eight wedding cakes contracted, and the food to prepare for three of these weddings. Preparations were quite detailed and began weeks ahead. We froze as many things as we could, and shined all of the silver in anticipation of "The Day." I had three wonderful crews headed up by Joan Holland, Joyce Nabors and Amanda Littrell going out to serve the wedding food and a driver delivering cakes starting early in the morning. I should have suspected that this day would be a real "lulu" when I discovered my driver had left for Huntsville with the wrong wedding cake. I jumped into my car, with the right cake, and roared to Huntsville, to the Heritage Club, swapped the cakes and headed back to Johnston Street to pack for another wedding. While I was gone, the crew, who had an 11:00 wedding in Huntsville, loaded cakes and food in the van for their assignment. All of this went very smoothly. I had no sooner arrived back at Johnston Street when my driver darted in the back door carrying a smashed wedding cake (the one I had swapped at Heritage Club), that was supposed to be in Madison. He had had a slight wreck, but the cake had "hit the deck." I spent the next hour repairing the cake and then sent it on. In the meantime, the second crew had left with their wedding food and wedding cakes for their destination. We were packing the last items in the van for the last wedding, to be at 5:30, when I heard a crash. The same driver that had been causing calamities all day, had closed the back of the van on two crystal bowls filled with marinated shrimp and artichokes. I wanted to cry. I think I did, I was so tired. But not for long. I sent the crew on to the wedding, and called Family Mart to see if they had any fresh shrimp—they did. I then prepared more artichokes, onions, and marinade, plopped it in a lucite bowl and sped to Family Mart, and picked up my shrimp. I arrived at the reception site fifteen minutes before guests arrived. All was saved. Another day in the life of a tired, frazzled caterer and restaurateur. A caterer must be resourceful, innovative, fast, and "crazy." I went home and collapsed. I have included some of the favorite recipes that we used at Johnston Street Cafe during the last ten years in our restaurant as well as the catering events. Johnston Street Cafe is now owned by Scott and Meg Curry. Scott is a talented young chef who not only plans to be open during the day, but is now opening for dinner.

Bacon and Cheese Crepes

1 small onion, finely chopped
1 tablespoon butter
2 cups shredded sharp
   Cheddar cheese
6 slices crisp-cooked bacon,
   crumbled
2 teaspoons brown spicy
   mustard
1/2 teaspoon Worcestershire
   sauce
1 tablespoon mayonnaise
18 (5½-inch) crepes

Sauté the onion in butter in a small skillet until tender. Combine the sautéed onion with the cheese, bacon, mustard, Worcestershire sauce and mayonnaise in a bowl and mix well. Divide the mixture into 18 portions. Shape each into a 4-inch log. Place a log on each crepe and roll up to enclose the filling. Arrange seam side down in a greased baking pan. Bake at 375 degrees just until the cheese melts. Cut each crepe into 3 pieces to serve as hors d'oeuvres and arrange on a serving plate.

Yield: 54 hors d'oeuvres

Hot Chicken Wings

8 cups margarine
4 bottles Tony's hot sauce
2 cups fresh lemon juice
12 tablespoons Tabasco sauce
10 teaspoons dried oregano
2 tablespoons dried basil
1 tablespoon dried marjoram
4 teaspoons dried rosemary
4 teaspoons dried thyme
4 teaspoons garlic salt
200 chicken wings

Combine the first 10 ingredients in a saucepan and simmer for several minutes or until well blended. Let stand until cool. Rinse the chicken wings, drain well and pat dry. Place the wings in a large container and add the marinade, mixing to coat well. Marinate the wings in the refrigerator for 3 hours or longer. Drain the wings, reserving the marinade. Arrange the wings in a single layer in foil-lined baking pans. Brush generously with the reserved marinade. Bake at 400 degrees for 15 minutes. Brush with reserved marinade. Bake for 15 to 20 minutes longer or until the wings are crispy. Arrange the wings on serving platters.

Yield: 200 chicken wings

Jackie Guice, a wonderful cook and friend, and I love to get together and chat about food. This crepe recipe is one the two of us did while teaching a cooking class together. Jackie is the author of When the Knead Rises, a super bread cookbook. We both attended the University of Tennessee.

Day Lily

Whole flowers or petals of the orange and yellow varieties can be eaten, but avoid the buds, which are bitter. Sweet, delicate taste. Stuff with herbed cheeses, or use in Chinese stir-fries or Japanese tempura.

Goat Cheese Rellenos

This recipe was given to me by Chef Greg Werb of Johnston Street Cafe.

20 Anaheim green chiles

15 ounces Monterey Jack cheese with jalapeños, shredded

9 ounces Montrachet goat cheese

1 tablespoon minced lightly roasted garlic

$1/4$ cup finely chopped green onions

$1/2$ cup chopped red or yellow bell pepper

1 tablespoon minced fresh cilantro

2 tablespoons minced Italian parsley

1 tablespoon minced fresh basil

$3/4$ teaspoon dried oregano

$1/2$ teaspoon minced blanched jalapeño

$1/2$ teaspoon salt

$1/4$ teaspoon white pepper

Rinse the chiles, pierce with a fork and arrange in a single layer on a baking sheet. Roast at 400 degrees until the skins blister, turning as necessary. Place the chiles in a large bowl, cover with damp paper towels and let stand until cool. Chill in the refrigerator. Remove the skins carefully, leaving the stems intact. Make a small slit in the side of each chile and remove the seeds. Combine the Monterey Jack cheese, Montrachet cheese, garlic, green onions, red bell pepper, cilantro, parsley, basil, oregano, jalapeño, salt and white pepper in a bowl and mix well. Stuff the chiles with the cheese mixture and arrange on a tray. Freeze until firm and place in sealable plastic bags. Store in the freezer until ready to use. Thaw and heat on a parchment-lined baking sheet until hot. Prepare the cheese mixture 1 day in advance to allow the flavors to marry and store, covered, in the refrigerator.

Yield: 20 servings

Shrimp Squares

4 cups fine whole-grain bread
  crumbs
$1/2$ cup grated Parmesan cheese
1 cup melted butter
4 cups shredded Swiss cheese
4 cups thinly sliced scallions
6 cups small cooked shrimp
24 eggs
4 teaspoons cornstarch
6 cups milk
Grated nutmeg to taste
Cayenne to taste
$1/4$ cup grated Parmesan cheese

Combine the bread crumbs, $1/2$ cup Parmesan cheese and melted butter in a bowl and mix well. Press the mixture evenly over the bottom of 4 greased 7x11-inch baking pans. Layer the Swiss cheese, scallions and shrimp over the crumb mixture and pat firmly. Beat the eggs in a large bowl. Add the cornstarch and beat until blended. Add the milk and beat until well mixed. Add the nutmeg and cayenne. Pour over the layers. Sprinkle with the remaining $1/4$ cup Parmesan cheese. Bake at 400 degrees for 15 minutes. Reduce the oven temperature to 350 degrees. Bake for 15 minutes longer. Cool for 20 minutes or longer. Cut the baked layer in each pan into 24 squares.

Yield: 96 servings

Zingy Tortilla Bites

24 ounces cream cheese,
  softened
2 cups sour cream
10 green onions, chopped
Juice of $1/2$ lime
1 to 4 jalapeños, seeded,
  finely chopped
1 (2-ounce) can chopped black
  olives, drained (optional)
$1^1/2$ cups mayonnaise
Salt and pepper to taste
20 large flour tortillas
1 (16-ounce) jar medium
  picante sauce

Blend the cream cheese and sour cream in an electric mixer or processor. Add the next 7 ingredients and mix well. Spread the cream cheese mixture on each tortilla and roll up tightly as for jelly roll. Place the tortilla rolls on a tray and cover tightly with a damp towel and plastic wrap to prevent drying. Chill for 8 to 10 hours. Cut the tortilla rolls into $1/2$- to $3/4$-inch slices and arrange on a serving platter. Serve with the picante sauce.

Yield: 10 dozen

One of our most "asked for" catering items was our tortilla bites when the men would order. A zippy filling and tortillas served with salsa or picante sauce. My friend, Jo Hosey, was always so good to come down at anytime and "rescue" me. She rolled many of these and helped with a number of other things.

Shrimp Paste

Keep cans of shrimp on the pantry shelf. This is so easy. Stuff the Shrimp Paste in chou puffs, brouchees, cherry tomatoes, and Belgian endive.

4 cups shredded Cheddar cheese
2 cans small shrimp, drained
1¹/₂ cups mayonnaise
2 tablespoons grated onion

Combine the cheese, shrimp, mayonnaise and onion in a large bowl and mix with a fork or an electric mixer until well mixed.

Yield: 3 cups

Amaretto Cream Dip

16 ounces cream cheese, softened
2 cups confectioners' sugar
¹/₄ cup amaretto
1 teaspoon almond flavoring
¹/₂ cup whipping cream
1 cup slivered almonds, toasted (optional)

Combine the cream cheese, confectioners' sugar, amaretto, almond flavoring and whipping cream in a mixer bowl. Beat until blended, scraping the bowl occasionally. Stir in the almonds. Serve with assorted fresh fruit.

Yield: 2¹/₂ cups

Vidalia Onion Baked Dip

3 large Vidalia onions, coarsely chopped
2 tablespoons unsalted butter
2 cups shredded Swiss cheese
2 cups mayonnaise
¹/₂ teaspoon Tabasco sauce
1 clove of garlic, minced
1 (8-ounce) can sliced water chestnuts
¹/₄ cup white wine

Sauté the onions in butter in a large skillet until tender. Combine the cheese, mayonnaise, Tabasco sauce, garlic, water chestnuts and wine in a large bowl. Add the sautéed onions and mix well. Spoon into a buttered casserole. Bake at 375 degrees for 25 minutes. Serve with tortilla chips and crackers.

Yield: 4 cups

Pesto

3¹/₄ cups lightly packed fresh basil leaves
1¹/₂ cups freshly grated Parmesan or Romano cheese
¹/₂ cup olive oil
5 tablespoons pine nuts
Salt and pepper to taste

Combine the basil, Parmesan cheese and olive oil in a blender or food processor container. Process until smooth and well blended. Stir in the pine nuts and season with salt and pepper. Pesto may also be used on hot pasta for a wonderful entrée or added to pizza, scrambled eggs, etc.

Yield: 1¹/₂ cups

Layered Cheese Torta with Pesto

This is so pretty. Once I prepared a gigantic cheese torta using 15 pounds of cream cheese for Kitty Caddell's wedding reception. It was a big torta!

24 ounces cream cheese,
   softened
24 ounces unsalted butter,
   softened (do not substitute)
Pesto (page 108)
Basil sprigs
Thin French bread slices
Bite-size crisp fresh vegetables

Combine the cream cheese and butter in a large mixer bowl and beat until very smooth and creamy. Line a 10-cup straight-sided plain mold, such as a tall brioche, charlotte or loaf pan or a clean flowerpot, with plastic wrap, draping the excess plastic wrap over the rim. Spread about $1/8$ of the cream cheese mixture in the prepared mold, extending to the side of the mold. Add a layer of about $1/7$ of the Pesto. Repeat the layers ending with the cream cheese mixture. (Make thicker or thinner layers if desired but divide the cream cheese mixture and Pesto into the desired number of portions before beginning to layer and be sure to begin and end with cream cheese mixture.) Fold the ends of the plastic wrap over the top layer and press lightly to compact the layers. Refrigerate for 1 to $1^1/2$ hours or until firm. Uncover the top layer and invert the torta onto a serving plate. Remove the plastic wrap carefully. Cover the torta with plastic wrap and refrigerate for up to 5 days. Garnish the torta with basil sprigs and serve with French bread and fresh vegetables.

Yield: 20 to 25 servings

Caponata

We served this at the Grand Princess Gala as one of the appetizers. It was a great hit. The Princess Theater has a warm place reserved in my heart because, when we arrived in Decatur, it was one of the first places I took my children.

2 medium eggplant
2 cups chopped onions
7 tablespoons olive oil
1¹/₃ cups thinly sliced celery
2 red bell peppers, chopped
2 teaspoons chopped garlic
1 (28-ounce) can tomatoes, coarsely chopped
¹/₃ cup wine vinegar
2 tablespoons sugar
¹/₄ cup tomato paste
¹/₂ cup chopped fresh parsley
1 teaspoon pepper
³/₄ cup sliced stuffed green olives
¹/₄ cup capers

Cut the unpeeled eggplant into 1-inch cubes. Sauté the eggplant and onions in olive oil in a large skillet until light golden brown. Add the celery, red bell peppers, garlic, undrained tomatoes, vinegar, sugar, tomato paste, parsley, pepper, olives and capers and mix well. Simmer, covered, for 30 minutes, stirring occasionally. Simmer, uncovered, for 10 minutes or until thickened to the desired consistency. Let stand until cool. Serve at room temperature to spread on French bread slices or for dipping with bagel chips. Caponata can also be served as a salad on lettuce-lined salad plates. It can be stored in the refrigerator for up to 2 weeks.

Yield: 4 cups

Savory Smoked Salmon Cheesecake

*This is a popular item for cocktail parties. Do you
ever get enough smoked salmon?*

2 tablespoons (about) butter

1/3 cup fine bread crumbs

1/4 cup Parmesan cheese

1 medium onion, finely
chopped

1 tablespoon bacon drippings

28 ounces cream cheese,
softened

4 eggs

1/2 cup cream

8 ounces bacon, crisp-fried,
crumbled

4 ounces smoked salmon,
shredded

2 or 3 drops of Tabasco sauce

Salt and freshly ground pepper
to taste

Cover the outside bottom of a watertight 8-inch
springform pan with foil. Coat the side and
bottom of the pan with the butter; sprinkle with
the bread crumbs and Parmesan cheese. Sauté
the onion in bacon drippings in a skillet until
clear and set aside. Combine the cream cheese,
eggs and cream in a large mixer bowl and beat
until smooth and creamy. Add the sautéed
onion, bacon, salmon, Tabasco sauce, salt and
pepper and mix well. Spoon into the prepared
pan. Place the springform pan in a larger pan.
Add boiling water to the larger pan to a depth
of 2 inches. Bake at 300 degrees for 1 hour
and 40 minutes. Let stand until cool. Store,
covered, in the refrigerator until serving time.
Remove the rim before serving.

Yield: 8 large servings, or 20 small servings

Lemon Sandwiches

*Cut seeded, peeled lemons
into very thin slices
and sandwich between
buttered thinly sliced whole
meal bread. Serve with
smoked salmon.*

Scallops and Champagne

This recipe is festive and a super chafing dish item. It can also be served over rice as an entrée.

1/4 cup butter
1/2 cup chopped shallots
1 bay leaf
1/4 teaspoon salt
1/4 teaspoon pepper
2 pounds scallops
1 1/2 cups dry Champagne
1 pound fresh mushrooms, sliced
2 tablespoons butter
1/4 cup all-purpose flour
2 cups crème fraîche
Juice of 1 lemon
1 tablespoon chopped fresh tarragon
1/4 cup chopped chives
2 teaspoons paprika
Cayenne to taste

Melt 1/4 cup butter in a large skillet. Add the shallots, bay leaf, salt and pepper and sauté until golden brown. Rinse the scallops and remove the side muscle. Cut the scallops into fourths if large. Add the Champagne and scallops to the skillet and simmer until the scallops are barely cooked. Drain the scallops, reserving the liquid. Sauté the mushrooms in 2 tablespoons butter in a second skillet until tender. Sprinkle with the flour and mix well. Cook for 2 to 3 minutes, stirring constantly. Add the crème fraîche and the reserved Champagne liquid and stir until well mixed. Stir in the lemon juice. Cook over low heat until thickened, stirring constantly. Add the scallops, tarragon and chives. Adjust the seasonings. Pour the mixture into a chafing dish. Sprinkle with the paprika and cayenne. Serve with toasted bread triangles and cocktail picks.

Yield: 1 1/2 quarts

Don't discard squeezed-out fruit. Rub over copper pans and basins with a little salt to make them shine.

Strawberry Colada Punch

1 (16-ounce) package frozen strawberries, thawed
1 (15-ounce) can cream of coconut
3 cups pineapple juice, chilled
3 cups club soda, chilled
2 cups rum (optional)

Combine the strawberries and cream of coconut in a blender and process until smooth. Pour the mixture into a pitcher. Stir in the pineapple juice, club soda and rum. Serve over crushed ice.

Yield: 2 1/2 quarts

Sunset Punch

4 cups cranberry juice cocktail
4 cups pink lemonade
4 cups orange juice
4 cups pineapple juice
4 cups ginger ale, chilled
1 quart raspberry sherbet
  or sorbet

Combine the cranberry juice, lemonade, orange juice and pineapple juice in a punch bowl. Stir in the ginger ale gently. Scoop the sherbet into the punch. Serve immediately.

Yield: 1¹/₂ gallons

Autumn Harvest Punch

2 cups water
1¹/₂ to 2 cups sugar
4 cinnamon sticks
36 whole cloves
8 cups cranberry juice cocktail
4 cups orange juice
1¹/₂ to 2 cups lemon juice
1 lemon, sliced
1 orange, sliced
1 cup rum, or 2 tablespoons
  rum extract

Combine the water, sugar, cinnamon and cloves in a large heavy saucepan. Bring to a boil over high heat, stirring until the sugar dissolves. Reduce the heat and simmer for 7 minutes. Remove from heat and discard the cinnamon and cloves. Stir in the cranberry juice, orange juice, lemon juice, lemon and orange slices and rum. Heat to serving temperature over medium heat.

Yield: 5 quarts

Golden Fruit Punch

2 tea bags
²/₃ cup boiling water
1¹/₂ cups pineapple juice
1 cup grapefruit juice
1 cup orange juice
¹/₂ cup lemon juice
1¹/₄ cups sugar
4 cups ginger ale, chilled
2 cups ice water

Steep the tea bags in boiling water in a covered container for 5 minutes. Discard the tea bags. Combine the tea, pineapple juice, grapefruit juice, orange juice and lemon juice in a large pitcher. Add the sugar and stir until the sugar dissolves. Chill until serving time. Stir in the ginger ale and ice water. Serve immediately.

Yield: 2¹/₂ quarts

Corn Chowder

2 tablespoons unsalted butter
8 ounces kielbasa, chopped
1 medium onion, chopped
4 ribs celery, including the
   leaves, chopped
2 pounds unpeeled red
   potatoes, chopped
2 quarts (or more) chicken
   stock
24 ounces frozen Shoe Peg
   corn, or kernels from 5 ears
   of corn
4 cups half-and-half
1/4 cup unsalted butter
1/2 cup flour
Salt and pepper to taste
1/2 cup chopped fresh parsley

Melt 2 tablespoons butter in a Dutch oven. Add the sausage, onion and celery. Sauté until the vegetables are tender. Add the potatoes. Add enough water or chicken stock to cover completely. Simmer, covered, for 8 to 10 minutes. Add the corn and stir to mix. Simmer, covered, for 10 minutes. Add the half-and-half. Cook until almost at the boiling point. Melt 1/4 cup butter in a small skillet. Add the flour. Cook until smooth, stirring constantly. Whisk the flour mixture (roux) into the chowder. Cook over medium-high heat until thickened. Season with salt and pepper. Serve in individual bowls or a tureen. Sprinkle with the parsley. Serve with Fried Tortilla Strips if desired.

Yield: 4 to 6 servings

This recipe for Corn Chowder was a "Taste of the Valley" award winner. There were many requests for this soup. Johnston Street Cafe won the best overall presentation for several years. Edwina Rice and I made many gallons of this through the years.

Fried Tortilla Strips

Corn or flour tortillas
Vegetable oil for frying

Cut the tortillas into thin strips. Fry in 360-degree oil in a skillet or deep fryer until golden brown; drain. Serve with your favorite soup. May add sour cream and thinly sliced jalapeños to complete this tasty garnish.

Yield: Variable

Sour Cream Mushroom Soup

This recipe, which is easy on your waistline, was given to me by Peggy Burkhart of Lexington, Kentucky, an old friend from medical school days.

1½ teaspoons canola oil
1 large onion, chopped
1½ teaspoons chopped fresh
   tarragon, or
   ½ teaspoon dried
1 pound mushrooms, trimmed,
   sliced
½ cup flour
3½ cups defatted beef broth
1 cup reduced-fat sour cream
1 cup skim milk
¼ teaspoon freshly grated
   nutmeg
Salt and freshly ground pepper
   to taste
Pinch of cayenne or dash of
   Tabasco sauce
Fresh chives (optional)
Fresh tarragon sprigs (optional)

Heat the canola oil in a large heavy saucepan over low heat. Add the onion. Cook for 5 to 7 minutes or until tender and translucent, stirring frequently. Add the tarragon. Cook for 1 minute, stirring frequently. Stir in the mushrooms. Cook, covered, for 5 minutes or until the mushrooms release their moisture. Sprinkle the flour over the mushrooms. Cook over medium heat for 3 to 4 minutes, stirring constantly. Stir in the beef broth gradually, scraping up any flour that clings to the saucepan. Simmer for 5 to 7 minutes or until thickened and smooth, stirring occasionally. Whisk in a mixture of the sour cream and milk. Season with the nutmeg, salt, pepper and cayenne. Heat gently until hot but not boiling, stirring constantly. Garnish with fresh chives and fresh tarragon sprigs.

Yield: 7 cups

Spicy Roasted Tomato Soup

*Yes, this is good. When I was in Westport, Connecticut, at a seminar
at Martha Stewart's farm, Turkey Hill, we had this soup for her mom's birthday
luncheon. By the way, Martha's family is just great—so is Martha—or was
when I was there for two seminars with only 22 participants for a week on two
different occasions. Carolyn Tweedy, Ann Pollard, and I felt like we
knew her well—she **is** a perfectionist.*

2¹/₂ quarts chicken stock
6 large onions, chopped,
    sautéed
4 red peppers, sliced, sautéed
2 quarts canned tomatoes,
    drained, chopped, or 6 large
    tomatoes, peeled, seeded,
    coarsely chopped
6 cloves of garlic, peeled,
    chopped
2 pounds carrots, peeled,
    chopped
2 tablespoons curry powder
Salt and pepper to taste
3 roasted red peppers, sliced

Bring the chicken stock to a boil in a stockpot.
Add the onions, 4 red peppers, tomatoes, garlic
and carrots. Cook until the vegetables are
tender, stirring occasionally. Season with the
curry powder, salt and pepper. Pour into a
blender container. Process until puréed. Ladle
into soup bowls. Top each serving with sliced
roasted peppers. To roast peppers, heat over an
open gas flame until blistered on all sides. Place
the peppers in a paper bag immediately; fold
down top of bag to enclose peppers. Let stand
until cool. Peel, seed and chop the peppers
when cool.

Yield: 3 quarts

Skinny Soup

2 cups chopped okra
1/2 cup chopped celery
1/2 cup shredded cabbage
1 (28-ounce) can chopped
    tomatoes
1/2 cup each chopped carrots,
    onion and cauliflower
3 quarts chicken stock
1 teaspoon basil
2 teaspoons Worcestershire
    sauce
1/4 teaspoon each thyme,
    marjoram and oregano
Salt and pepper to taste

Combine the okra, celery, cabbage, tomatoes, carrots, onion, cauliflower, chicken stock, basil, Worcestershire sauce, thyme, marjoram, oregano, salt and pepper in a medium stockpot. Simmer for 30 minutes. Add additional beef or chicken stock if needed.

Yield: 12 to 15 servings

We always served this Skinny Soup so that those on a diet could enjoy it without adding the dreaded fat grams. If you prefer, use a bag of chopped oriental vegetables instead of the carrots, celery and cauliflower. Our stock at Johnston Street was relatively fat-free as we only cooked the chicken tenders from which the fat was stripped.

Cajun Soup

*This soup is spicy, has a wonderful flavor, and is low in fat.
What more could you want on a cold evening?*

2 quarts stewed tomatoes
3 quarts chicken stock
2 pounds boneless skinless
    chicken strips, cut into
    chunks
Flour
Vegetable oil
2 (10-ounce) packages frozen
    okra
3 cups deveined peeled shrimp
1 tablespoon Creole seasoning,
    or to taste

Purée the tomatoes in a food processor. Heat the tomatoes and chicken stock in a large stockpot. Coat the chicken with flour. Brown in the oil in a skillet. Add to the tomato mixture. Cook until the chicken is cooked through. Add the okra. Cook until the okra is hot. Add the shrimp. Cook for 15 minutes or until the shrimp turn pink. Stir in the Creole seasoning.

Yield: 12 to 15 servings

The Johnston Street Cafe

Chicken Mushroom Tarragon Soup

5 pounds boneless chicken
2 cups butter
2 pounds mushrooms, sliced
3 large onions, finely chopped
1 cup chopped celery
2 cups flour
4 cups cream
Butter
1 teaspoon tarragon, or to taste
White pepper to taste

Rinse the chicken. Cook the chicken in salted water to cover in a stockpot until cooked through, about 30 minutes. Drain, reserving 12 cups of the stock. Cut the chicken into chunks, discarding the skin. Heat 2 cups butter in a large stockpot over medium heat until melted. Sauté the mushrooms, onions and celery in the stockpot. Whisk in the flour until blended. Stir in the cream gradually. Cook until bubbly, stirring constantly. Add the reserved stock and mix well. Cook until thickened, stirring constantly. Stir the tarragon, white pepper and chicken into the cream sauce. Add enough additional stock until of the consistency of whipping cream. Cook until heated through, stirring constantly.

Yield: 1 gallon

Wisconsin Cheddar Cheese Soup

This soup has a wonderful flavor and was a popular one with JSC customers.

1/4 cup butter
1/2 cup chopped carrots
1/2 cup diced green bell pepper
1/2 cup minced onion
1/3 cup flour
4 cups rich chicken stock
6 ounces medium Wisconsin
   Cheddar cheese, shredded
6 ounces aged Wisconsin
   Cheddar cheese, shredded
Salt and pepper to taste
Milk (optional)

Melt the butter in a 3-quart saucepan. Add the carrots, green pepper and onion. Sauté until the vegetables are tender but not brown. Add the flour and mix well. Add the chicken stock. Cook until thickened, stirring constantly. Add the cheeses, stirring constantly. Season to taste. Simmer for 15 minutes. May thin with a small amount of milk.

Yield: 1 quart

Congealed Waldorf Salad

This is so delicious. Mr. John Caddell, one of my favorite people and a longtime supporter of Johnston Street Cafe, declared this his favorite salad.

½ envelope unflavored gelatin
¼ cup cold water
1 (8-ounce) can juice-pack crushed pineapple
2 eggs, beaten
½ cup sugar
⅛ teaspoon salt
¼ cup lemon juice
2 unpeeled apples, cored, finely chopped
½ cup finely chopped celery
½ cup broken pecans or walnuts
½ cup whipping cream, whipped

Soften the gelatin in the cold water and mix well. Drain the pineapple, reserving ½ cup juice. Reserve ½ cup pineapple. Combine the reserved pineapple juice, eggs, sugar, salt and lemon juice in a double boiler and mix well. Cook over hot water until thickened, stirring constantly. Stir in the gelatin mixture. Let stand until cool. Add the apples, celery, reserved pineapple and pecans. Fold in the whipped cream. Spoon into a lightly oiled 5-cup mold or into 10 custard cups sprayed with nonstick cooking spray. Chill until set.

Yield: 10 servings

Pesto Potato Salad

4 cups chopped peeled cooked potatoes
1½ cups cubed Wisconsin Monterey Jack cheese
½ cup chopped celery
½ cup sliced green onions
½ cup chopped red bell pepper
1 cup mayonnaise
2 tablespoons Pesto (page 108)
1 tablespoon grated Wisconsin Parmesan cheese

Combine the potatoes, Monterey Jack cheese, celery, green onions and red bell pepper in a bowl and mix gently. Add a mixture of the mayonnaise and Pesto, tossing lightly to coat. Sprinkle with the Parmesan cheese. Chill, covered, until serving time.

Yield: 6 servings

A tablespoon of lemon juice will acidulate water sufficiently to prevent vegetables such as sweet potatoes and Jerusalem artichokes from discoloring. Similarly, sprinkle cut avocados, apples and bananas with a little lemon juice to help prevent them from discoloring too.

Fresh Vegetable Salad

Colorful and very tasty! This was one of the more popular salads in the deli case at Johnston Street Cafe.

1½ cups vegetable oil
1 cup sugar
½ cup vinegar
2 tablespoons poppy seeds
2 teaspoons dry mustard
1 small onion, grated
4 stalks broccoli, cut into
    bite-size pieces
Florets of 1 small head
    cauliflower, cut into
    bite-size pieces
8 large mushrooms, sliced
1 medium green bell pepper,
    chopped
3 ribs celery, chopped

Combine the oil, sugar, vinegar, poppy seeds, dry mustard and onion in a quart jar with a tightfitting lid. Shake until mixed. Combine the broccoli, cauliflower, mushrooms, green pepper and celery in a bowl and mix gently. Add the oil mixture, tossing to coat. Marinate, covered, in the refrigerator for 3 hours or up to 2 days before serving, stirring occasionally.

Yield: 8 to 10 servings

Nasturtium

Spicy, peppery flowers—nasturtiums—add vitality and color to a wide variety of salads. Colors range from bright yellow and orange to vivid red. Their taste reminds some of radishes.

Cold Pea Salad

The crunch of the cashews is like the icing on a cake.

1 (10-ounce) package frozen
    peas
1 cup chopped celery
¼ cup chopped scallions
1 teaspoon chopped fresh
    dillweed, or ¼ teaspoon
    dried dillweed
½ cup sour cream
Salt to taste
¼ teaspoon white pepper
1 cup cashews

Combine the peas, celery, scallions and dillweed in a bowl and mix well. Add the sour cream, salt and pepper, stirring until mixed. Chill, covered, until serving time. Add the cashews to the salad just before serving.

Yield: 4 to 6 servings

Poppy Seed Dressing

*Everyone raves about this dressing which happens to be the dressing
we served over our fresh fruit. Most people think the strawberries in the salad
give the dressing the red color, but it is merely food coloring.*

4¹/₂ cups sugar
2 cups vinegar
3 tablespoons onion juice
2 tablespoons dry mustard
2 tablespoons salt
6 cups salad oil
3 tablespoons poppy seeds
¹/₂ teaspoon red food coloring

Combine the sugar, vinegar, onion juice, dry
mustard and salt in a mixer bowl. Beat at
medium speed until blended. Add the oil
gradually, beating constantly until blended.
Stir in the poppy seeds and food coloring.

Yield: 10 cups

Rotini Salad with Bacon and Cheese

¹/₂ cup olive oil
¹/₄ cup red wine vinegar
2 teaspoons raspberry vinegar
Salt and freshly ground pepper
   to taste
12 ounces rotini or fusilli
1 cup freshly grated Parmesan
   cheese
¹/₄ cup finely chopped fresh
   parsley, chives, basil and/or
   tarragon
8 ounces bacon, crisp-fried,
   crumbled

Combine the olive oil, wine vinegar, raspberry
vinegar, salt and pepper in a jar with a tightfitting lid and shake to blend. Cook the pasta
using package directions until al dente; drain.
Rinse with cold water and drain. Toss the pasta,
cheese and fresh herbs in a bowl. Add ³/₄ of
the dressing, tossing to coat. Let stand at
room temperature for 30 minutes to allow
the flavors to marry. Add the bacon and the
remaining dressing just before serving. Adjust
the seasonings. May substitute a mixture of
¹/₄ cup olive oil and ¹/₄ cup salad oil for the
olive oil and chopped fresh parsley for the
mixed fresh herbs.

Yield: 6 servings

Mexican Egg Salad

12 hard-cooked eggs, chopped
1¹/₂ cups shredded Cheddar
  cheese
4 ribs celery, chopped
5 scallions, sliced
2 jalapeños, minced
1 red bell pepper, chopped
1 clove of garlic, minced
1 cup (about) mayonnaise
Juice of 1 lime
1 tablespoon cumin
1 tablespoon chili powder
Salt and pepper to taste
Chopped fresh coriander
Avocado slices
Lime juice

Combine the eggs, cheese, celery, scallions, jalapeños, red bell pepper and garlic in a bowl and mix well. Combine the mayonnaise, lime juice, cumin and chili powder in a bowl and mix well. Fold into the egg mixture, adding additional mayonnaise if needed to bind the salad. Season with salt and pepper. Spoon into a serving bowl. Chill, covered, for several hours to allow flavors to marry. Top with coriander and avocado slices sprinkled with lime juice. May substitute 5 green onions with 2 inches of tops for scallions.

Yield: 10 to 12 servings

This egg salad is a super stuffing for most anything. We kept this in the deli case when we had time to chop all the ingredients. Use as a stuffing in cherry tomatoes, as a topping for foccacia or in puff pastry cups topped with caviar. Good flavor and just a little spicy.

Thousand Island Dressing

We use this dressing as a base for many different dishes. You might recognize it as the dressing for our Turkey Deluxe Sandwich.

3 medium green bell peppers,
  finely chopped
8 ribs celery, finely chopped
2 large onions, finely chopped
5 cups mayonnaise
2¹/₂ cups sour cream
2 (12-ounce) jars chili sauce
1 tablespoon Worcestershire
  sauce
1¹/₂ teaspoons salt
Pepper to taste

Combine the green peppers, celery and onions in a bowl. Stir in a mixture of the mayonnaise, sour cream, chili sauce, Worcestershire sauce, salt and pepper. Store, covered, in the refrigerator.

Yield: 14 cups

White Bean and Goat Cheese Salad

An unusual but very tasty salad.

1 pound dried small white
   beans
6 cups chicken stock,
   homemade if possible
3 carrots, peeled, chopped into
   1/4-inch pieces
2 bay leaves
1/3 cup fresh lemon juice
1 1/2 tablespoons coarse Dijon
   mustard
2 cloves of garlic, minced
1 1/4 cups olive oil
Salt and freshly ground pepper
   to taste
12 ounces Montrachet cheese,
   crumbled
1 medium red onion, chopped
1/2 cup pine nuts, toasted
1 bunch parsley, chopped

Sort and rinse the beans. Combine the beans with enough water to cover in a bowl. Let stand for 8 to 10 hours; drain. Combine the beans, chicken stock, carrots and bay leaves in a stockpot. Bring to a boil; reduce heat. Skim off any foam that rises to the surface. Simmer for 25 to 30 minutes or until the beans are tender; drain. Discard the bay leaves. Combine the lemon juice, Dijon mustard and garlic in a bowl and mix well. Add the olive oil gradually, whisking constantly until mixed. Season with salt and pepper. Add the warm beans, tossing to coat. Stir in the cheese, onion, pine nuts and parsley. Serve at room temperature.

Yield: 8 to 10 servings

Honey French Dressing

This is a tasty honey French dressing and very easy to prepare. This recipe was given to me years ago by my great friend, Katherine Wilks, who co-edited Cotton Country Cooking with me. This dressing is also known as the Johnston Street Cafe House Dressing.

2 cups sugar
2 cups catsup
1 cup vegetable oil
1 cup cider vinegar
1 tablespoon lemon juice
   (optional)
2/3 teaspoon salt
1 onion, grated

Combine the sugar, catsup, oil, vinegar, lemon juice, salt and onion in a food processor container. Process until smooth.

Yield: 2 pints

Blintz Soufflé

1¹/2 cups sour cream
¹/2 cup orange juice
¹/2 cup butter or margarine,
    softened
1 cup flour
¹/3 cup sugar
6 eggs
2 teaspoons baking powder
Cream Cheese Filling
Sour cream
Blueberry syrup and/or
    assorted jams

Combine 1¹/2 cups sour cream, orange juice, butter, flour, sugar, eggs and baking powder in a blender or food processor container fitted with a metal blade. Process until blended. Spread ¹/2 of the batter in a buttered 9x13-inch baking dish. Drop the Cream Cheese Filling by heaping spoonfuls over the prepared layer. Spread evenly with a knife; it will mix slightly with the batter. Top with the remaining batter. Bake at 350 degrees for 50 to 60 minutes or until puffed and golden. Serve immediately with additional sour cream and blueberry syrup and/or assorted jams. May prepare several hours to 1 day in advance and store, covered, in the refrigerator. Bring to room temperature before baking.

Yield: 8 servings

Cream Cheese Filling

8 ounces cream cheese,
    softened
2 cups small-curd cottage
    cheese
1 egg
1 tablespoon sugar
1 teaspoon vanilla extract

Combine the cream cheese, cottage cheese, egg, sugar and vanilla in a food processor container fitted with a metal blade. Process until blended. May blend with an electric mixer.

Stuffed Crepes for Twelve

1/2 cup butter
1/2 cup minced green onions
2 pounds fresh lump crab meat
1/8 teaspoon garlic powder
    (optional)
Salt and pepper to taste
1/2 cup vermouth
2/3 cup vermouth
1/4 cup milk
1/4 cup cornstarch
4 cups whipping cream
2 1/2 cups (or more) shredded
    Swiss cheese
24 crepes
Butter

Heat 1/2 cup butter in a skillet until melted. Stir in the green onions. Add the crab meat and mix well. Cook for several minutes, stirring constantly. Season with garlic powder, salt and pepper. Stir in 1/2 cup vermouth. Bring to a boil. Boil until most of the liquid has been absorbed. Spoon into a bowl. Bring 2/3 cup vermouth to a boil in the same skillet. Boil until reduced to 2 tablespoons. Remove from heat. Stir in a mixture of the milk and cornstarch. Add the whipping cream gradually and mix well. Season with salt and pepper. Cook over low heat until slightly thickened, stirring constantly. Add 1 1/2 cups of the cheese and mix well. Cook until blended, stirring constantly. Combine 1/2 of the cheese sauce with the crab meat mixture and mix well. Spoon a heaping spoonful of the mixture onto each crepe; roll to enclose the filling. Arrange seam side down in 2 buttered 9x13-inch baking dishes. Spoon the remaining cheese sauce over the crepes; sprinkle with the remaining 1 cup cheese. Dot with butter. Chill, covered, in the refrigerator. Remove from the refrigerator 30 minutes before baking. Bake at 400 degrees for 20 minutes or until bubbly. May be frozen but must be thawed before baking.

Yield: 12 (2-crepe) servings

For a fancy lunch, prepare these crepes in advance and freeze. Always use fresh crab meat if available. It does get a little tiring flipping all those crepes, but the end result will be well worth the effort.

Sausage Casserole

Great for breakfast, brunch or Sunday night supper.
Serve with fresh fruit and lemon yogurt.

8 slices bread, crusts trimmed
1 pound sausage
1 cup chopped red or green bell
    pepper
1 teaspoon prepared mustard
1 cup shredded Swiss cheese
1/2 cup shredded Cheddar
    cheese
1 cup milk
3 eggs, lightly beaten
3/4 cup light cream ·
1 teaspoon Worcestershire
    sauce
1/4 teaspoon salt
1/8 teaspoon pepper

Arrange the bread over the bottom of a buttered 9x13-inch baking dish. Sauté the sausage and bell pepper in a skillet, stirring until the sausage is crumbly; drain. Stir in the prepared mustard. Spoon over the prepared layer; sprinkle with the Swiss cheese and Cheddar cheese. May freeze at this point for future use. Combine the milk, eggs, light cream, Worcestershire sauce, salt and pepper in a bowl, beating until blended. Pour over the prepared layers. Bake at 350 degrees for 30 to 35 minutes or until set.

Yield: 10 servings

Fresh Fruit Salsa

There's nothing like fresh salsa to complement fresh fish,
chicken or pork, or Sausage Casserole.

1 1/2 cups chopped fresh
    pineapple
2 cups chopped tomatoes
1/2 cup chopped red bell pepper
1/2 cup chopped yellow bell
    pepper
1/2 cup chopped purple onion
1/4 to 1/2 cup chopped cilantro
1/4 cup chopped seeded jalapeños
Juice of 1 lime
Juice of 1 lemon
2 cloves of garlic, minced
Salt to taste

Combine the pineapple, tomatoes, red bell pepper, yellow bell pepper, onion, cilantro, jalapeños, lime juice, lemon juice, garlic and salt in a bowl and mix gently. Serve chilled or at room temperature. Wear rubber gloves to protect your skin when handling hot peppers.

Yield: 3 cups

Baked Bananas

This is a good brunch dish, but is also a wonderful accompaniment to curried chicken or any other curry dish.

4 ripe bananas
1/4 cup unsalted butter
2 tablespoons dry sherry
1 tablespoon lime juice
1/3 cup loosely packed brown sugar
1 teaspoon cinnamon

Cut the bananas crosswise into halves; cut lengthwise into halves. Arrange in a single layer in a 9x11-inch baking dish. Heat the butter in a saucepan over medium heat until melted. Stir in the sherry and lime juice. Cook just until heated through. Pour over the bananas. Sprinkle with the brown sugar and cinnamon. Bake at 375 degrees for 12 to 15 minutes or until light brown and bubbly.

Yield: 8 servings

Goat Cheese and Green Onion Scones

Wonderful with beef instead of a roll for appetizers at your next cocktail party.

2 cups unbleached flour
1 tablespoon baking powder
1 teaspoon salt
1/2 teaspoon ground pepper
4 ounces soft mild goat cheese, crumbled, chilled
3 large green onions, thinly sliced
3/4 cup half-and-half
1 egg

Combine the flour, baking powder, salt and pepper in a bowl and mix well. Add the cheese and green onions, stirring with a fork to mix. Beat the half-and-half and egg in a bowl until blended. Add to the flour mixture, stirring until the mixture forms a ball. Roll into a 3/4-inch-thick round on a lightly floured surface; cut with a biscuit cutter. Arrange on a baking sheet. Bake at 375 degrees for 25 minutes or until brown. Let stand for 10 minutes. Serve warm.

Yield: 12 servings

Orange Mint Salsa

Sections of 2 oranges, seeded, chopped
3 kiwifruit, finely chopped
1/4 cup snipped fresh mint
1/4 cup minced red onion
1 teaspoon grated orange zest
Salt to taste

Combine the oranges, kiwifruit, mint, onion, orange zest and salt in a bowl and mix well. Chill, covered, until serving time. May serve at room temperature.

Yield: 1 1/2 cups

Banana Bread

*My wonderful employee, Edwina Rice, who was with me before I opened
Johnston Street made thousands of loaves of this bread. It is very moist.*

1/2 cup butter
1 cup sugar
2 eggs
1 teaspoon vanilla extract
1 cup mashed bananas
1/2 cup chopped pecans
1/2 cup sour cream
1 1/2 cups flour
1 teaspoon baking soda
1/2 teaspoon salt
Orange Cream Cheese Filling

Combine the butter, sugar, eggs, vanilla,
bananas, pecans, sour cream, flour, baking soda
and salt in the order listed in a mixer bowl,
mixing well after each addition. Beat for 1
minute. Spoon into a greased and floured
5x9-inch loaf pan. Bake at 350 degrees for
1 hour. Invert onto a wire rack to cool. Slice
and spread with Orange Cream Cheese Filling.

Yield: 1 medium loaf

Orange Cream Cheese Filling

This is the mystery filling for the banana bread sandwich.

16 ounces cream cheese,
    softened
3/4 cup confectioners' sugar
Grated peel of 1 orange
2 tablespoons frozen orange
    juice concentrate

Beat the cream cheese in a mixer bowl until
light and fluffy. Add the confectioners' sugar,
orange peel and orange juice concentrate,
beating until blended.

Yield: 2 cups

Pumpkin Bread

Every fall we switched from our banana bread sandwich filled with Orange Cream Cheese Filling (page 128) to a pumpkin bread sandwich. We used this sandwich on the chicken salad plate to accompany the chicken salad, fresh fruit with poppy seed dressing and a homemade sweet pickle. This bread is very moist and has a wonderful flavor.

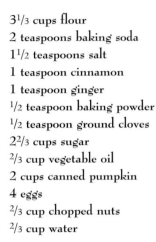

3^1/$_3$ cups flour
2 teaspoons baking soda
1^1/$_2$ teaspoons salt
1 teaspoon cinnamon
1 teaspoon ginger
^{1}/$_2$ teaspoon baking powder
^{1}/$_2$ teaspoon ground cloves
2^2/$_3$ cups sugar
^{2}/$_3$ cup vegetable oil
2 cups canned pumpkin
4 eggs
^{2}/$_3$ cup chopped nuts
^{2}/$_3$ cup water

Sift the flour, baking soda, salt, cinnamon, ginger, baking powder and cloves into a bowl and mix well. Combine the sugar, oil, pumpkin, eggs and nuts in a bowl and mix well. Add the flour mixture, stirring until blended. Stir in the water. Spoon into three 1-pound loaf pans or two 1^1/$_2$-pound loaf pans. Bake at 350 degrees for 1 hour. Let stand until cool. Slice and spread with Orange Cream Cheese Filling.

Yield: 3 (1-pound) loaves, or
2 (1^1/$_2$-pound) loaves

To welcome a new neighbor, place a loaf of home-baked Banana or Pumpkin Bread in an attractive basket, arrange colored cellophane around it, and tie it all together with pretty ribbons or raffia.

The Best Blueberry Muffins

We served these and kept them available in the deli case at Johnston Street Cafe for many years. This is the best I've ever tasted. Actually, I prefer adding all of the blueberries at the end of preparation...unless, of course, you like blue muffins. Annie Cheatam, a good employee, made hundreds of these.

$^1/_2$ cup butter, softened
1 cup (or less) sugar
2 eggs
2 teaspoons baking powder
1 teaspoon vanilla extract
$^1/_4$ teaspoon salt
$^1/_2$ cup blueberries, mashed
2 cups flour
$^1/_2$ cup milk
2 cups blueberries
1 tablespoon sugar
$^1/_4$ teaspoon nutmeg

Grease 12 muffin cups including the area between each cup or line muffin cups with foil baking cups. Beat the butter in a mixer bowl until creamy. Add 1 cup sugar or less depending on the tartness of the blueberries, beating until pale yellow and fluffy. Add the eggs 1 at a time, beating well after each addition. Add the baking powder, vanilla and salt and mix well. Stir in $^1/_2$ cup mashed blueberries. Fold in $^1/_2$ of the flour and $^1/_2$ of the milk. Add the remaining flour and milk and mix well. Fold in 2 cups blueberries. Spoon into the prepared muffin cups. Sprinkle with a mixture of 1 tablespoon sugar and nutmeg. Bake at 375 degrees for 25 to 30 minutes or until golden brown. Cool in muffin cups for 30 minutes or longer.

Yield: 12 muffins

Oat Bran Muffins

Honey Glaze for Bran Muffins
7¹/₂ cups flour
2 tablespoons cinnamon
2 tablespoons baking powder
4¹/₂ teaspoons baking soda
1 teaspoon ground cloves
5 cups oat flakes
2 cups rolled oats
2 cups oat bran
6 cups applesauce
4 cups packed dark brown
   sugar
3 cups skim milk
1 cup vegetable oil
6 egg whites
Oat Topping

Brush the sides and bottoms of the muffin cups generously with the Honey Glaze for Bran Muffins. Sift the flour, cinnamon, baking powder, baking soda and cloves into a bowl and mix well. Combine the oat flakes, oats and oat bran in a bowl and mix well. Stir in the flour mixture. Combine the applesauce, brown sugar, skim milk, oil and egg whites in a bowl and mix well. Add to the flour mixture, stirring just until moistened; do not overmix. Spoon into the prepared muffin cups. Sprinkle with the Oat Topping. Bake at 350 degrees for 15 minutes or until the muffins test done.

Yield: 40 muffins

Honey Glaze for Bran Muffins

¹/₂ cup butter, softened
¹/₂ cup sugar
¹/₂ cup packed brown sugar
5 tablespoons honey
3 tablespoons boiling water

Beat the butter, sugar and brown sugar in a mixer bowl until light and fluffy, scraping the bowl occasionally. Add the honey and boiling water, beating until blended.

Oat Topping

1¹/₂ cups rolled oats
¹/₂ cup margarine, softened
¹/₂ cup packed dark brown
   sugar
1 teaspoon cinnamon

Combine the oats, margarine, brown sugar and cinnamon in a bowl and mix well.

I was the official taster for these muffins. We were rarely without these Oat Bran Muffins as I ate at least one a day and sometimes two. These muffins have no cholesterol.

This Focaccia is so simple to make in a food processor. The rising time is short and it makes a terrific bread to serve as an accompaniment to a meal or as bread for a grilled veggie sandwich. Top Focaccia with grilled veggies and mozzarella cheese, broil briefly, and voilà, a delicious treat.

Focaccia

1 envelope dry yeast
³/₄ cup lukewarm water
2 cups flour
¹/₂ teaspoon salt
¹/₄ cup olive oil
Sliced or quartered green and
    black olives
Fresh snipped herbs, especially
    rosemary
Thinly sliced onions
Shaved prosciutto or ham
Sliced mushrooms
Pine nuts (optional)

Dissolve the yeast in the lukewarm water and mix well. Let stand for 5 minutes. Combine the flour and salt in a food processor container fitted with a blade for dough or a metal blade. Add the yeast mixture and 3 tablespoons of the olive oil. Process until the flour is absorbed. May be mixed by hand. Knead on a lightly floured surface for 2 minutes or until smooth and elastic, adding additional flour as needed to form an easily handled dough. Place the dough in a greased bowl, turning to coat the surface. Let rise, covered with plastic wrap, in a warm place for 1 hour or until doubled in bulk. Punch the dough down. Let rest for 5 minutes. Pat into a 10-inch round on a greased pizza pan or into a 9x13-inch rectangle on a baking sheet; pull the dough apart in several places to form small holes. Brush with the remaining 1 tablespoon olive oil. Sprinkle with olives, herbs, onions, prosciutto and mushrooms. Let rise, covered, for 15 minutes. Bake at 425 degrees for 20 to 25 minutes or until golden brown. Cool in pan on a wire rack. May sprinkle with pine nuts just before serving.

Yield: 1 (10-inch) round flat loaf

Refrigerator Rolls

This roll mix keeps for 3 days in the refrigerator. I make orange rolls and caramel rolls with this basic recipe.

1 cup water
1/2 cup butter or margarine
1/2 cup shortening
3/4 cup sugar
1 1/2 teaspoons salt
1 cup lukewarm water
2 envelopes dry yeast
2 eggs, lightly beaten
6 cups (about) flour
Melted butter

Bring 1 cup water to a boil in a saucepan. Remove from heat. Add 1/2 cup butter and shortening, stirring until melted. Stir in the sugar and salt. Let stand until lukewarm. Pour 1 cup lukewarm water into a large bowl. Sprinkle the yeast over the water; stir until dissolved. Stir the butter mixture and eggs into the yeast mixture. Add just enough flour to make a stiff dough and mix well. Chill, covered, for 8 to 10 hours. Roll 1/4 to 1/3 inch thick on a lightly floured surface. Cut with biscuit cutter; fold in half. Place in a greased baking pan. Brush with melted butter. Let rise in a warm place for 1 1/2 to 2 hours. Bake at 400 degrees for 12 to 15 minutes or until brown. May cut and shape as desired.

Yield: 8 dozen rolls

Grilled Peppered Tenderloin of Beef

This is Doctor Bill's specialty.

1 (6- to 7-pound) fillet of beef
1 cup olive oil
1/2 cup red wine
Cracked pepper to taste
2 cloves of garlic, minced
  (optional)

Place fillet in shallow dish. Pour mixture of olive oil, red wine, pepper and garlic over beef, turning to coat. Marinate, covered, in the refrigerator for 1 hour, turning occasionally. Rub with additional cracked pepper. Grill on gas grill on High for 5 minutes; turn over the beef. Grill on High for 5 minutes. Reduce temperature to Medium. Grill for 20 minutes longer or until a meat thermometer registers 140 degrees for rare or 160 degrees for medium. Let stand for 10 minutes before slicing.

Yield: 10 to 12 servings

Refresh Your Microwave

Slice a lemon and float the slices in a bowl of water. Microwave on High for 4 to 5 minutes. Wipe the microwave with paper towels.

Prize-Winning Meat Loaf

This is the famous meat loaf served every Wednesday at Johnston Street Cafe with smashed potatoes, slaw, broccoli or squash casserole and Edwina's corn bread.

1 1/2 pounds ground chuck
1 cup milk
3/4 cup chopped onion
1/2 cup fine dry bread crumbs
1 egg, lightly beaten
2 tablespoons catsup
1 teaspoon salt
1/4 teaspoon pepper
1/8 teaspoon paprika
2 tablespoons catsup

Combine the ground chuck, milk, onion, bread crumbs, egg, 2 tablespoons catsup, salt, pepper and paprika in a bowl and mix well. Shape into a long flat loaf in a 9x12-inch baking pan or fit into a loaf pan. Spread 2 tablespoons catsup evenly over top of loaf. Bake at 375 degrees for 40 minutes or until cooked through. May add 1/2 teaspoon mixed herbs and 1/2 teaspoon dry mustard to enhance flavor. May microwave on High for 15 to 20 minutes, turning 3 times.

Yield: 6 servings

Rack of Lamb with Herb Mustard Glaze

Rack of lamb is one of my most favorite entrées. My mother often served leg of lamb for Sunday dinner in the spring of the year. She would stud the lamb with garlic cloves, sprinkle with salt and pepper and bake to perfection, serving the finished product with mint jelly. You could use the Herb Mustard Glaze on a leg of lamb.

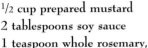

$^{1}/_{2}$ cup prepared mustard

2 tablespoons soy sauce

1 teaspoon whole rosemary, crushed

$^{1}/_{4}$ teaspoon ginger

1 clove of garlic, minced

1 egg

2 tablespoons olive oil

2 (2$^{1}/_{2}$-pound) lamb roasts, 8 ribs each

Combine the prepared mustard, soy sauce, rosemary, ginger, garlic and egg in a blender container. Process for 15 seconds or until smooth. Add the olive oil in a fine stream, processing constantly on High for 30 seconds or until light and creamy. Trim the exterior fat on the lamb roasts to within $^{1}/_{4}$ inch. Arrange the lamb fat side up on a rack in a shallow roasting pan. Brush the mustard mixture over the roasts. Bake at 375 degrees for 45 minutes or until a meat thermometer registers 140 degrees for rare, 160 degrees for medium or to the desired degree of doneness.

Yield: 6 to 8 servings

Lavender

Blue-purple lavender flowers are wonderful when used sparingly in soups, sorbets, jellies, or ice cream, or to augment poultry and quail dishes.

French Roast Chicken

This is very simple but delicious. One of my favorites!
The tarragon gives a great flavor.

1 (3¹/₂- to 4-pound) roasting chicken
¹/₄ cup unsalted butter
3 sprigs of tarragon
2 cups (or more) chicken stock

Rinse the chicken and pat dry. Rub the inside cavity with 1 tablespoon of the butter and tarragon; truss. Rub the remaining 3 tablespoons of butter over the outside of the chicken. Pour 1 cup of the chicken stock into a roasting pan. Arrange the chicken breast side up in the roasting pan. Bake at 400 degrees for 20 minutes; baste with the pan drippings. Turn the chicken on its side. Bake for 20 minutes and baste. Turn the chicken on the other side. Bake for 20 minutes. If the chicken is not cooked through, turn the chicken on its back. Bake for 10 minutes longer. Remove the chicken to a serving platter. Skim the pan drippings. Deglaze with the remaining 1 cup stock. Cook until thickened and of sauce consistency, stirring constantly. Carve the chicken and drizzle with the sauce. To truss the chicken, wrap string around the tail, then around the legs, up the back, over the wings and tie behind. Tuck the wing tips back. May bake the chicken without trussing.

Yield: 4 to 5 servings

Chicken and Dumplings

A much sought after item at Johnston Street Cafe in the winter months. Barbara Griffin made these so delicious.

1 large hen
Perfect Pie Pastry
Salt and pepper to taste
4 quarts chicken stock

Rinse the hen. Combine the hen with enough water to cover in a stockpot. Cook until tender. Drain, reserving 4 quarts of the stock. Chop the chicken, discarding the skin and bones. Bring the reserved stock to a simmer in the stockpot. Roll the Perfect Pie Pastry on a heavily floured surface. Cut into small squares. Drop the pastry squares into the simmering stock. Cook for 20 minutes or until the dumplings are firm. Stir in the chicken. Season with salt and pepper.

Yield: 15 servings

Perfect Pie Pastry

2 cups flour
1/2 teaspoon salt
3/4 cup unsalted butter, chilled
1/4 cup ice water

Combine the flour and salt in a food processor container. Process for several seconds. Add the butter. Process until crumbly. Add the ice water gradually, processing just until blended. Chill, covered, for 30 minutes or longer. This recipe will make two 9-inch pie shells.

Marinated Baked Chicken Breasts

These chicken breasts hold well and make an excellent entrée for lunch or dinner. We sent these out on many catering events.

12 boneless chicken breasts
2 cups sour cream
1/4 cup lemon juice
4 teaspoons Worcestershire
    sauce
1 tablespoon salt
2 teaspoons celery salt
2 teaspoons paprika
1 teaspoon pepper
1/2 teaspoon garlic salt
1 1/2 cups butter cracker crumbs
1 1/2 cups saltine cracker crumbs
1 cup melted margarine

Rinse the chicken and pat dry. Combine the sour cream, lemon juice, Worcestershire sauce, salt, celery salt, paprika, pepper and garlic salt in a shallow dish and mix well. Add the chicken, turning to coat. Chill, covered, for 8 to 10 hours, turning occasionally. Roll the chicken in a mixture of the butter crackers and saltine crackers. Arrange in a shallow baking pan. Drizzle with 1/2 of the margarine. Bake at 300 degrees for 1 hour. Drizzle with the remaining margarine. Bake for 45 minutes longer or until cooked through. May use low-fat sour cream and low-fat cracker crumbs.

Yield: 12 servings

Lemon juice is a valuable source of Vitamin C; whenever possible, avoid destroying this by adding lemon juice to dishes after they have cooked.

Cheezy Chicken

One of the favorite entrées served for lunch at Johnston Street Cafe. Meg Petty was always happy when this dish was on the menu.

12 ounces vermicelli or flat egg
    noodles
16 ounces Velveeta, shredded
16 ounces mushrooms, sliced
2 small green bell peppers,
    chopped
2 onions, chopped
1/4 cup butter
8 boneless skinless chicken
    breast halves, cooked,
    chopped
2 (10-ounce) cans tomatoes
    with chiles, drained

Cook the pasta using package directions; drain. Combine the hot pasta and Velveeta in a bowl, stirring until the cheese melts. Sauté the mushrooms, green peppers and onions in the butter in a skillet until tender. Stir into the pasta mixture. Add the chicken and tomatoes and mix well.

Yield: 8 to 10 servings

Chicken Crab Artichoke Divan

Serve at your next luncheon with marinated asparagus,
baked stuffed tomatoes and hot rolls.

2 (10-ounce) packages frozen
 artichoke hearts, thawed,
 drained
4 whole skinless chicken breasts,
 split, boned
1/4 cup butter
6 to 7 ounces fresh crab claw
 meat
1/4 cup dry sherry
Salt and pepper to taste
3 tablespoons butter
1 cup sliced mushrooms
1/4 cup finely chopped onion
3 tablespoons flour
1 1/3 cups whipping cream
1 cup milk
1/2 cup chopped fresh parsley
1/8 teaspoon cayenne
1/4 cup grated Parmesan cheese
Paprika to taste

Arrange the artichokes in a buttered 8x12-inch baking dish. Rinse the chicken and pat dry. Sauté in 1/4 cup butter in a skillet for 15 minutes. Stir in the crab meat. Cook for 5 minutes. Add the sherry and mix well. Cook until the sherry is absorbed. Season with salt and pepper. Remove the chicken and crab meat with a slotted spoon to a platter, reserving the pan drippings. Cover to keep warm. Add 3 tablespoons butter to the reserved pan drippings and mix well. Sauté the mushrooms and onion in the butter mixture until tender. Sprinkle with the flour and stir until mixed. Add the whipping cream and milk and mix well. Cook until thickened, stirring constantly. Stir in the parsley and cayenne. Remove from heat. Stir in the cheese. Spoon 1/2 of the cheese sauce over the artichokes. Arrange the chicken and crab meat over the prepared layers. Top with the remaining cheese sauce. Sprinkle with paprika. Bake at 375 degrees for 20 minutes. Serve over hot cooked rice. May be prepared up to 3 days in advance, stored in the refrigerator and baked just before serving. Bring to room temperature before baking.

Yield: 8 servings

Chicken Pie with Puff Pastry

One of my favorite entrées that was sold from the "take-out" case.
This is a recipe given to me or adapted from Bonnie Bailey's recipe. We could
not make this often enough or make enough of it. It disappeared quickly
from the kitchen as the hot "entrée of the day."

3 pounds boneless skinless
   chicken breasts
Salt to taste
1 medium onion
1 rib celery
1 carrot
1¹/₂ cups butter
2¹/₂ cups flour
2¹/₂ cups chicken stock
2 quarts milk
¹/₂ cup white wine
¹/₂ cup butter
2 cups mushrooms
2 cups chopped celery
2 cups chopped carrots
1 cup chopped onion
1 (17-ounce) package puff
   pastry

Rinse the chicken. Combine the chicken, salt, 1 onion, 1 rib celery and 1 carrot with enough water to cover in a stockpot. Cook for 45 minutes or until tender. Drain, discarding the vegetables. Cut the chicken into 2-inch pieces. Heat 1¹/₂ cups butter in a saucepan until melted. Add the flour, whisking until blended. Add the stock, whisking constantly. Stir in the milk and white wine. Cook until thickened and of a sauce consistency, stirring constantly. Heat ¹/₂ cup butter in a heavy saucepan until melted. Add the mushrooms, 2 cups celery, 2 cups carrots and 1 cup onion. Sweat the vegetables, covered, over low heat for 15 minutes; drain. Stir into the cream sauce. Add the chicken and mix well. Spoon the chicken mixture into two 3-quart baking dishes sprayed with nonstick cooking spray. Top each with a sheet of puff pastry, sealing the edges. Prick the top of the pastry with a fork or cut slits. Bake at 400 degrees until puffed and brown.

Yield: 24 servings

Chicken la Verle

4 pounds chicken breasts
2 (6-ounce) packages long grain
    and wild rice
3 or 4 onions, chopped
16 ounces mushrooms, sliced
1 cup butter
1 1/2 cups milk
1 (10-ounce) can cream of
    chicken soup
1 (10-ounce) can cream of
    mushroom soup
16 ounces sharp Cheddar
    cheese, shredded
Salt and pepper to taste

Combine the chicken with enough water to cover in a stockpot. Cook until tender; drain. Shred the chicken. Prepare the rice using package directions using 1 of the seasoning packets. Sauté the onions and mushrooms in the butter in a skillet until tender. Stir in the milk and soup. Cook until of sauce consistency, stirring constantly. Add the rice, cheese, salt and pepper and mix well. Layer the chicken and cheese sauce alternately in a baking dish until all ingredients are used, ending with the cheese sauce. Bake at 300 to 350 degrees until bubbly.

Yield: 12 to 14 servings

Chicken Supreme Casserole

One of Johnston Street Cafe's most favorite "take-out" entrées.

2 to 3 cups chopped cooked
    chicken
2 cups cooked rice
1 1/2 cups chopped celery
1 small onion, chopped
4 hard-cooked eggs, chopped
1 (3-ounce) package slivered
    almonds
2 (10-ounce) cans cream of
    mushroom soup
1 cup mayonnaise
2 tablespoons lemon juice
1 teaspoon salt
1 cup bread crumbs
2 tablespoons margarine

Combine the chicken, rice, celery, onion, eggs and almonds in a bowl and mix gently. Add a mixture of the soup, mayonnaise, lemon juice and salt and mix well. Spoon into a buttered 9x12-inch baking pan. Brown the bread crumbs in the margarine in a skillet. Sprinkle over the prepared layer. Chill, covered, for 8 to 10 hours. Remove from refrigerator 1 hour before baking. Bake at 350 degrees for 40 to 45 minutes or until brown and bubbly.

Yield: 8 to 10 servings

Chicken la Verle just brings to mind Johnston Street Cafe, since it was one of our more popular entrées for lunch as well as catered events. India Harris, a good cook and one of my managers, made this often.

Lemon Chicken

A noontime favorite at Johnston Street Cafe. My friend Pat Owens, who often helped out at the cafe, loves this dish. Serve at room temperature at a tailgate party.

4 pounds boneless skinless chicken breast halves, cut into strips
2 cups fresh lemon juice
2 cups flour
2 teaspoons salt
2 teaspoons paprika
1 teaspoon freshly ground pepper
1/2 cup corn oil
2 tablespoons grated lemon zest
1/4 cup packed brown sugar
1/4 cup chicken stock
1 teaspoon lemon extract
2 lemons, sliced paper thin

Rinse the chicken and pat dry. Mix the chicken and lemon juice in a bowl just large enough to hold the mixture. Marinate, covered, in the refrigerator for 2 hours, turning occasionally. Drain and pat dry. Combine the flour, salt, paprika and pepper in a sealable plastic bag and shake to mix. Shake the chicken 2 pieces at a time in the bag until coated with the flour mixture. Heat the corn oil in a skillet until hot. Fry the chicken in several batches for 10 minutes per batch or until brown and crisp; drain. Arrange the chicken in a single layer in a shallow baking pan. Sprinkle with the lemon zest and brown sugar. Pour a mixture of the stock and lemon extract over the chicken. Top each piece with a lemon slice. Bake, covered with foil, at 350 degrees for 20 minutes; remove the foil. Bake for 10 minutes longer. May substitute chicken tenders for the chicken breasts.

Yield: 10 to 12 servings

To extract the maximum amount of juice from a lemon, bring to room temperature and then roll on a work surface a few minutes before squeezing. Alternatively, microwave on High for 30 seconds, which warms the fruit, yielding more juice.

Poppy Seed Chicken

*An easy luncheon dish with a fancy presence when served with
spiced cold fruit, bread and dessert.*

5 whole chicken breasts,
  cooked, chopped
2 (10-ounce) cans cream of
  chicken soup
1 cup sour cream
1 sleeve butter flavor crackers,
  crushed
1/2 cup melted butter
2 tablespoons poppy seeds

Arrange the chicken in a lightly greased 9x13-inch baking dish. Combine the soup and sour cream in a bowl and mix well. Spread over the chicken; sprinkle with the cracker crumbs. Drizzle with the butter and sprinkle with the poppy seeds. Bake at 350 degrees for 20 to 25 minutes or until bubbly.

Yield: 8 servings

Shrimp Jambalaya

*A favorite recipe I obtained many years ago from my friend,
Penny Trammell. We served this dish practically every Friday as the
"to go" entrée at the Johnston Street Cafe.*

8 slices bacon
2 medium onions, chopped
1 cup chopped celery
1 large green bell pepper,
  chopped
1 cup rice
2 cups beef bouillon
2 tablespoons New Orleans hot
  sauce
2 tablespoons Worcestershire
  sauce
1 bay leaf
Seasoned salt and pepper
  to taste
1 pound peeled shrimp

Fry the bacon in a skillet until crisp. Drain, reserving the bacon drippings. Crumble the bacon. Pour just enough of the reserved bacon drippings into a skillet to measure 1/4 inch. Sauté the onions, celery and green pepper in the bacon drippings until tender. Stir in the rice. Sauté until light brown. Bring the bouillon to a boil in a saucepan. Add the bouillon, hot sauce, Worcestershire sauce, bay leaf, seasoned salt, pepper and bacon and mix well. Cook until the rice is tender, stirring occasionally. Add the shrimp and mix well. Cook for 10 minutes or until the shrimp turn pink; do not overcook the shrimp. Discard the bay leaf.

Yield: 6 servings

Baked Lemon Shrimp with Garlic

*Why not serve this with a green salad, French bread and your
favorite dessert. This is one of our favorites to prepare on ski
trips to Breckenridge with the Coughlins, our dear friends from Knoxville.
Actually it is a recipe prepared for us by Eydie and Gene Swanson
from Mankato, Minnesota, our orthopedic buddies who ski with us, also.*

1 cup unsalted butter
1 1/2 teaspoons salt, or to taste
1 tablespoon minced garlic, or
   to taste
1/2 cup finely chopped flat-leaf
   parsley
2 pounds large shrimp, peeled
2 tablespoons freshly grated
   lemon zest
2 tablespoons fresh lemon
   juice, or to taste

Heat the butter and salt in an ovenproof baking
pan large enough to hold shrimp in a single
layer until melted. Stir in the garlic and 1/2 of
the parsley. Arrange the shrimp in a single layer
in the prepared pan. Bake at 450 degrees for
5 minutes; turn the shrimp. Sprinkle with
the remaining 1/4 cup parsley and lemon zest.
Drizzle with the lemon juice. Bake for 5 to 10
minutes longer or until the shrimp turn pink.
Serve with hot cooked rice and lemon wedges.

Yield: 6 servings

*Eliminate smells from
your refrigerator by
arranging four or five
lemon slices strategically
on the shelves and in the
door of an empty
refrigerator. Leave for
several hours before
removing.*

Crab Cakes

This is a recipe given to me by Scott Curry, the chef and new owner of Johnston Street Cafe. A good recipe with a minimum of preparation. Serve with fruit salsa, grilled asparagus and sweet potato fries, which are prepared just as white potato fries.

1 pound jumbo lump crab
  meat
3/4 cup mayonnaise
2 tablespoons fresh lemon juice
1 teaspoon salt
1/2 teaspoon ground white
  pepper
2 cups crushed saltine
  crackers
Butter

Remove any bone or cartilage from the crab meat. Leave the crab meat in lump form; do not tear. Combine the crab meat, mayonnaise, lemon juice, salt and white pepper in a bowl, stirring gently with a rubber spatula just until mixed. Shape into 2- to 2$\frac{1}{2}$-ounce patties. Coat with cracker crumbs. Sauté the crab cakes in butter in an ovenproof skillet until golden brown; turn. Bake at 300 degrees for 10 minutes.

Yield: 5 servings

Use the seeds and juice of a lemon when making jam. Lemon is a good source of pectin, which helps set jam with poor setting properties. The lemon also brings out the flavor of the fruit.

The Johnston Street Cafe

One of the most wonderful "old stand-bys" is this recipe for Lasagna. Easily prepared and may be frozen and pulled out for that unexpected family weekend supper. We tried all kinds of really gourmet entrées for lunch and in the "take-out," but the most popular were meat loaf and lasagna.

Lasagna

12 ounces lasagna noodles
1 tablespoon vegetable oil
Salt to taste
1 pound ground beef
1 (28-ounce) can stewed
    tomatoes
2 (6-ounce) cans tomato paste
1½ tablespoons sugar
1 tablespoon whole basil
1½ teaspoons salt
½ bay leaf, crushed
1 clove of garlic, minced
3 cups small-curd cottage
    cheese
¾ cup grated Parmesan cheese
    or Romano cheese
3 eggs, lightly beaten
2 tablespoons parsley flakes, or
    ¼ cup chopped fresh
    parsley
2 teaspoons salt
½ teaspoon pepper
10 slices mozzarella cheese

Bring a large saucepan of water to a boil. Add the noodles, oil and salt to taste. Cook for 12 minutes or until tender. Drain and rinse with cold water. Brown the ground beef in a skillet, stirring until crumbly; drain. Stir in the undrained tomatoes, tomato paste, sugar, basil, 1½ teaspoons salt, bay leaf and garlic. Simmer for 30 minutes, stirring occasionally. Combine the cottage cheese, Parmesan cheese, eggs, parsley flakes, 2 teaspoons salt and pepper in a bowl and mix well. Layer the noodles, cottage cheese mixture, mozzarella cheese and ground beef mixture ½ at a time in a deep baking dish sprayed with nonstick cooking spray. Bake at 350 degrees for 40 minutes. Let stand for 15 minutes before serving. Create a vegetarian lasagna by substituting drained thawed frozen chopped spinach or the vegetable of your choice for the ground beef mixture.

Yield: 12 servings

Pasta Milanaise

This is so good! Toby Sewell shared this recipe with me.

12 ounces angel hair pasta
1¹/₂ cups sliced fresh
   mushrooms
¹/₂ cup butter
2 tablespoons flour
2 cups half-and-half
1 cup milk
4 ounces Cheddar cheese,
   shredded
1¹/₂ cups ground ham
¹/₄ cup sherry
1 teaspoon white pepper
1 teaspoon onion juice
1 teaspoon oregano (optional)
1 clove of garlic, crushed
Salt to taste
1 cup grated Parmesan cheese

Cook the pasta using package directions; drain. Sauté the mushrooms in the butter in a saucepan. Add the flour and mix well. Add the half-and-half and milk gradually, stirring constantly. Cook until thickened, stirring constantly. Stir in the Cheddar cheese, ham, sherry, white pepper, onion juice, oregano, garlic and salt. Cook until the cheese melts, stirring frequently. Add the pasta and mix gently. Spoon into a 2¹/₂-quart baking dish. Sprinkle with the Parmesan cheese. Bake at 350 degrees for 30 minutes or until bubbly. May be prepared in advance, stored in the refrigerator and baked just before serving.

Yield: 8 servings

Broccoli Gourmet

2 (10-ounce) packages frozen
    chopped broccoli
1 (10-ounce) can cream of
    mushroom soup
2 tablespoons grated onion
2 eggs, beaten
1 cup shredded sharp Cheddar
    cheese
1 cup mayonnaise
Buttered bread crumbs

Cook the broccoli using the package directions, drain well and set aside. Combine the soup, onion, eggs, cheese and mayonnaise in a bowl and fold the ingredients together until well mixed. Layer the broccoli and soup mixture in a greased casserole. Top with the buttered crumbs. Bake at 350 degrees for 20 to 30 minutes or until heated through and golden brown.

Yield: 8 servings

This broccoli dish was served each Wednesday on "Meat Loaf Day" at Johnston Street Cafe. In the summer months we served yellow squash casserole because the squash was plentiful from my garden.

Marinated Carrots

Can any cookbook survive without a marinated carrot recipe? I love to serve this with marinated chicken breasts over rice.

2 pounds carrots
1 small green bell pepper,
    sliced
1 medium onion, sliced
1 (10-ounce) can tomato soup
1/2 cup vegetable oil
1 cup sugar
3/4 cup vinegar
1 teaspoon prepared mustard
1 teaspoon Worcestershire
    sauce
Salt to taste

Scrape the carrots and slice into circles or diagonally Chinese-style. Cook the carrots in boiling salted water until tender-crisp and drain well. Layer the cooked carrots, green pepper and onion in a large bowl. Combine the soup, oil, sugar, vinegar, mustard, Worcestershire sauce and salt in a medium bowl and mix well. Pour over the carrot mixture. Refrigerate overnight before serving.

Yield: 16 servings

Turmeric Tomatoes

Turmeric Tomatoes is a popular dish served now at Johnston Street Cafe by the new owner Scott Curry. Packed into attractive jars, these extremely potent, sweet and spicy tomatoes make lovely Christmas gifts.

1¹/₂ pounds tomatoes, peeled
1 bunch scallions, sliced
3 to 5 serrano chiles, sliced
³/₄ cup white vinegar
¹/₄ cup packed brown sugar
1 tablespoon coarse salt
2 tablespoons freshly grated
 gingerroot
2 tablespoons puréed or
 minced garlic
1 tablespoon black or yellow
 mustard seeds
1 tablespoon cracked black
 peppercorns
1 tablespoon ground cumin
2 teaspoons cayenne
1 teaspoon turmeric
³/₄ cup olive oil

Cut each tomato into 6 wedges and place in a large bowl. Add the scallions and chiles and set aside. Bring the vinegar to a boil in a small saucepan. Add the brown sugar and salt. Cook for 1 minute or until completely dissolved. Remove from the heat and set aside. Combine the gingerroot, garlic, mustard seeds, peppercorns, cumin, cayenne and turmeric in a small bowl. Heat the olive oil in a medium saucepan over moderate heat until smoking. Add the spice mixture. Cook for about 2 minutes or until the aromas are released, stirring constantly with a wooden spoon. Remove from the heat and stir in the vinegar mixture. Pour the mixture over the vegetables and mix gently. Refrigerate, covered with plastic wrap, for 3 days or longer.

Yield: 3 cups

Mango Salsa

When handling hot peppers, wear rubber gloves to protect your skin.

2 to 3 ripe mangoes, chopped
1 jalapeño, seeded, minced
¹/₄ cup minced red onion
¹/₄ cup chopped fresh cilantro
2 tablespoons cider vinegar
Salt to taste

Combine the mangoes, jalapeño, onion, cilantro, vinegar and salt in a bowl and mix well. Refrigerate, covered, until serving time. Serve chilled or at room temperature.

Yield: 1¹/₂ cups

Bring out the flavor of mangoes, papayas, and guavas by sprinkling with lemon juice.

Risotto with Champagne

1/4 cup butter
1 medium onion, minced
4 cups chicken broth
1 (16-ounce) package arborio
    rice
2 cups dry Champagne
1 cup whipping cream
1/2 cup freshly grated
    Parmesan cheese
5 fresh basil leaves, cut into
    thin strips
Grated Parmesan cheese
    to taste

Melt the butter in a medium saucepan. Add the onion. Cook, covered, over low heat for 20 minutes or until the onion is very soft. Bring the broth to a boil in a saucepan. Stir the rice into the onion mixture. Add some of the Champagne and 1 cup of the heated broth. Cook until the liquid is absorbed, stirring constantly. Add the remaining broth and Champagne 1 cup at a time. Cook after each addition until the liquid has been absorbed, stirring constantly. Stir in a mixture of the whipping cream and 1/2 cup Parmesan cheese. Remove from heat. Let stand, covered, for a few minutes. Spoon into a serving dish. Garnish with basil strips. Serve with grated Parmesan cheese to taste.

Yield: 8 servings

Calendula
(Pot Marigold)

*The small orange or
yellow flowers and petals
of the calendula add
dramatic color to salads,
winter squash, or carrot
soup, or rice.*

Pear Relish

This recipe came from my friend, Toby Sewell, my neighbor "across the way"
for many years. She not only shared her recipe but also shared
her pears. This recipe does demand a firm pear.

4 cups finely chopped unpeeled
    pears
4¹/₂ cups finely chopped white
    onions
3 cups sugar
12 green bell peppers (5 cups),
    finely chopped
¹/₂ cup finely chopped hot red
    or green peppers
3 cups vinegar
2 tablespoons salt
1¹/₂ teaspoons celery seeds

Combine the pears, onions, sugar, peppers, vinegar, salt and celery seeds in a large saucepan. Bring the mixture to a boil and reduce the heat. Simmer for 45 minutes, stirring frequently. Ladle into hot sterilized jars and seal with 2-piece lids. Process in a boiling water bath for 5 minutes.

Yield: 6 to 7 pints

Garlic Pickles

1 gallon sour pickles
1 bulb garlic
5 pounds sugar
¹/₄ cup mustard seeds
3 or 4 cinnamon sticks
¹/₄ cup black peppercorns

Drain the pickles and cut into ³/₄-inch slices. Place the pickle slices in a large pottery container or other non-reactive container. Separate the garlic bulb into cloves, peel and add to the pickles. Add the sugar, mustard seeds, cinnamon sticks and peppercorns and mix well. Let the pickles cure for 3 weeks, stirring daily.

Yield: 4 quarts

This pickle recipe is truly famous. There are people who would "die" for them. We could not keep these made. Be sure to get a sour pickle that does not have garlic or other ingredients besides the vinegar solution. We use Rodenberry sour pickles. Shannon Bailey stirred these pickles around for many years.

Honey-Poached Pears

10 pears
1/4 cup plus 2 tablespoons
   lemon juice
6 cups water
2 cups honey
4 (3-inch) cinnamon sticks
Whipping cream
Orange peel strips

Peel the pears, leaving the stems in place. Cut a thin slice from the bottom of each pear so they will stand upright. Brush with a small amount of lemon juice to prevent discoloration. Combine the water, remaining lemon juice, honey and cinnamon sticks in a large saucepan. Bring to a boil; reduce the heat. Stand the pears in the liquid. Poach, covered, for 15 to 25 minutes or until the pears are tender. Beat the whipping cream in a mixer bowl until soft peaks form. Spoon into a shallow serving dish. Stand the pears upright in the whipped cream. Garnish with orange strips. Serve immediately. May cook the pears in advance and refrigerate until serving time. Bring the liquid to a boil, then reduce the heat. Simmer the pears, covered, for 5 minutes or until heated through.

Yield: 10 servings

Bananas Foster

1 tablespoon butter
1/4 cup firmly packed dark
   brown sugar
1/8 teaspoon ground cinnamon
4 bananas, peeled, cut into
   quarters
1/4 cup banana liqueur
1/4 cup dark rum
12 ounces nonfat vanilla
   frozen yogurt

Melt the butter in a large skillet over medium-high heat. Add the brown sugar, cinnamon, bananas and banana liqueur. Cook for 2 minutes or until the bananas are softened, stirring constantly. Pour the rum over the bananas and ignite with a match. Cook until the flames subside, swirling the skillet. Serve immediately over the yogurt.

Yield: 4 servings

Banana Bread Pudding with Rum Sauce

1/3 cup raisins or currants

2 tablespoons plus 1/4 cup dark rum

2 tablespoons butter

3 bananas, peeled, halved crosswise, then lengthwise

5 tablespoons sugar

2 cups whipping cream or evaporated skim milk

4 eggs

1 teaspoon vanilla extract

8 ounces white bread slices

1/2 cup chopped toasted pecans

Rum Sauce (at right)

Soak the raisins in 2 tablespoons of the rum for 20 minutes. Melt the butter in a large heavy skillet over medium heat. Add the bananas; sprinkle with 2 tablespoons of the sugar. Simmer for 2 minutes on each side, or until the bananas are softened. Remove from the heat. Whisk the whipping cream, eggs, vanilla, remaining rum and remaining sugar in a mixer bowl until smooth. Trim the crusts from the bread and cut each slice into 3 strips. Arrange 1/3 of the bread crosswise in a buttered 5x9-inch loaf pan. Top with 6 slices of banana. Sprinkle with half the raisins and half the pecans. Arrange 1/3 of the remaining bread crosswise over the pecans. Pour half the cream mixture over the layers. Layer with the remaining bananas, raisins, pecans and bread. Pour in the remaining cream mixture, pressing gently with a spoon. Let stand for 15 minutes. Bake at 350 degrees for 45 minutes or until puffed and golden brown and knife inserted in center comes out clean. Cool in the pan on a wire rack. Slice the pudding and arrange on dessert plates. Drizzle with the Rum Sauce and serve.

Yield: 6 to 8 servings

Rum Sauce

1/4 cup unsalted butter

1/2 cup whipping cream

1/2 cup packed dark brown sugar

Pinch of salt

2 tablespoons dark rum

Melt the butter in a heavy medium saucepan over medium-high heat. Add the cream, brown sugar and salt. Bring to a boil, stirring until the sugar dissolves; remove from the heat. Stir in the rum. Serve warm.

Apricot Roses

Dip dried apricot halves in hot water to soften. Pat dry. Roll to 1/8-inch thickness, using a rolling pin. Wrap several apricot halves around the cone, pressing the sticky side inward. Curl the upper edges outward for a petal effect. Pinch the rose at the bottom for a stem.

Carrot Cake

The best carrot cake ever! We must have sold thousands of these.
I can see Edwina Rice now, icing these in the late afternoon.
They're still turning them out at JSC.

3 cups unbleached flour
3 cups sugar
1 teaspoon salt
1 tablespoon baking soda
1 tablespoon ground cinnamon
1½ cups corn oil
4 eggs, lightly beaten
1 tablespoon vanilla extract
1½ cups chopped pecans
1½ cups shredded coconut
1⅓ cups puréed cooked
   carrots
¾ cup drained crushed
   pineapple
Cream Cheese Frosting
Confectioners' sugar

Sift the flour, sugar, salt, baking soda and cinnamon into a large bowl. Add the oil, eggs and vanilla, beating well. Fold in the pecans, coconut, carrots and pineapple. Grease two 9-inch cake pans and line with waxed paper. Pour in the batter. Bake at 350 degrees on the middle rack of the oven for 30 to 35 minutes or until the cakes pull slightly away from the sides of the pans and the layers test done. Invert onto a wire rack and cool for 3 hours. Spread the tops of the layers with the Cream Cheese Frosting; stack the layers. Frost the side of the cake. Dust with confectioners' sugar.

Yield: 10 to 12 servings

Cream Cheese Frosting

8 ounces cream cheese,
   softened
6 tablespoons butter, softened
3 cups confectioners' sugar
1 teaspoon vanilla extract
Juice of ½ lemon (optional)

Cream the cream cheese and butter in a mixer bowl until light and fluffy. Sift in the confectioners' sugar, beating constantly. Stir in the vanilla and lemon juice.

Chocolate Cake

This is the chocolate cake I have used as one of the ingredients for the dome cake. My friend Bonnie Bailey in Birmingham made dome cakes at her Highland Gourmet Restaurant. The dome cake recipe was given to her by a friend. When Bonnie went out of business, she suggested that I make them, and I have. She even brought me the pans. Bonnie's recipe for "dome cake" is in her cookbook, Remembrances, *published in 1995. A great book.*

1 cup boiling water
4 ounces unsweetened
  chocolate
½ cup butter
2 cups cake flour, sifted
½ teaspoon salt
1 teaspoon baking soda
2 cups sugar
½ cup buttermilk
2 eggs, beaten
1 teaspoon vanilla extract
Chocolate Frosting

Pour the boiling water over the chocolate and butter to melt; cool and pour into a mixing bowl. Sift in the dry ingredients; beat at medium speed for 2 minutes. Add the buttermilk; beat for 2 minutes. Add the eggs and vanilla; beat for 2 minutes. Pour into a 9x13-inch pan or two 8-inch round cake pans. Bake at 350 degrees for 35 minutes or until the cake tests done. Frost the cake.

Yield: 12 servings

Chocolate Frosting

½ cup margarine
3 tablespoons baking cocoa
5 tablespoons milk
1 box sifted confectioners' sugar
1 teaspoon vanilla extract

Mix the margarine, baking cocoa and milk in a saucepan over medium heat. Bring to a boil, stirring constantly. Remove from the heat and beat in sugar. Add vanilla. Beat until of spreading consistency.

Chocolate Curls

Create quick and easy chocolate curls by cutting the sides of mint-filled chocolate candies with a vegetable peeler.

Citrus Curls with Mint

Using a citrus stripper, cut long strips from an orange or lemon. Curl strips around finger, then remove. Arrange curls together on one end, and allow other ends to curl freely. Add mint or other green herb.

Chocolate Roulage

6 ounces semisweet chocolate bits
3 to 4 tablespoons water
½ teaspoon instant coffee powder
5 to 6 egg yolks
¾ cup sugar
5 to 6 egg whites
Pinch of salt
Confectioners' sugar
1 cup whipping cream
Vanilla extract, rum or brandy to taste

Line the bottom of an 11x14-inch jelly roll pan with parchment paper or waxed paper. Combine the chocolate, water and coffee powder in a heavy saucepan. Cook over very low heat until the chocolate is melted, stirring until thick and creamy. Remove from the heat. Whisk the egg yolks and sugar in a bowl until thick and lemon colored. Add the cooled chocolate mixture, stirring well. Beat the egg whites and salt in a mixer bowl until stiff peaks form. Fold into the chocolate mixture. Spread the mixture into the prepared pan. Bake at 350 degrees for 20 to 25 minutes or until a wooden pick inserted near the center comes out clean. Cool to room temperature. Cover with a clean, damp cloth. Chill for 12 hours. Sprinkle with confectioners' sugar. Invert onto waxed paper; trim the edges. Beat the whipping cream in a mixer bowl until stiff peaks form. Fold in vanilla, rum or brandy to taste. Spread over the roulage. Roll up as for a jelly roll. Place on a serving plate. Sprinkle with confectioners' sugar or cocoa. Garnish with whipped cream.

Yield: 8 to 10 servings

Chocolate Chess Pie

Quick and easy. A great recipe to double, triple and put in the freezer for future use, for a gift, emergency dessert, or church supper. We've used this one a lot in our catering and in our pastry case "out front."

¼ cup melted margarine or
   unsalted butter
1½ cups sugar
3 tablespoons baking cocoa
1 (5-ounce) can evaporated
   milk
¼ teaspoon salt
2 eggs, beaten
1 teaspoon vanilla extract
1 unbaked (9-inch) pie shell

Combine the margarine, sugar, cocoa, evaporated milk, salt, eggs and vanilla in a bowl, beating well. Pour into the pie shell. Bake at 350 degrees for 30 minutes or until firm. Cool before serving.

Yield: 6 to 8 servings

CocoLocos

Great flavor! The cookies may be stored for up to one week in an airtight container.

1 cup unsalted butter, softened
⅔ cup packed light brown
   sugar
⅔ cup sugar
1 egg
1 teaspoon vanilla extract
1¾ cups flour
½ teaspoon baking soda
¼ teaspoon salt
8 ounces semisweet or
   bittersweet chocolate, cut
   into ½-inch pieces
1½ cups rolled oats
1 cup sweetened, grated
   coconut
½ cup coarsely chopped
   pecans

Cream the butter, brown sugar and sugar in a mixer bowl until light and fluffy. Add the egg and vanilla, beating well. Stir in the flour, baking soda and salt with a wooden spoon. Fold in the chocolate, oats, coconut and pecans. Spoon rounded tablespoonfuls of the dough onto a cookie sheet, leaving 2 inches between the cookies. Bake at 375 degrees for 12 minutes or until the cookies are golden brown. Cool on a wire rack.

Yield: 3 dozen cookies

Violet

Purple and pink violet blooms with a sweet, sometimes spicy flavor are often candied and used for garnish on cakes and desserts. The flowers, stems, and leaves are edible in salads and vinaigrettes.

Chocolate Chubbies

6 ounces semisweet chocolate, cut into small pieces

2 ounces unsweetened chocolate, cut into small pieces

5 tablespoons unsalted butter

3 eggs

1 cup (scant) sugar

1/4 cup flour

1/2 teaspoon (scant) baking powder

Pinch of salt

8 ounces semisweet chocolate chips

8 ounces broken-up pecans

8 ounces broken-up walnuts

Combine the semisweet and unsweetened chocolate pieces with the butter in a double boiler. Cook over hot water until the chocolate is melted, stirring frequently. Remove from the heat and let stand to cool slightly. Beat the eggs and sugar in a bowl until smooth. Add the cooled chocolate mixture, beating constantly. Sift the flour, baking powder and salt together into a bowl. Add to the chocolate mixture, stirring until moistened. Fold in the chocolate chips, pecans and walnuts. Drop the batter by tablespoonfuls onto 2 greased cookie sheets, leaving 2 inches between the cookies. Bake at 325 degrees for 15 to 20 minutes or until lightly browned.

Yield: 3 dozen large cookies

Lemon Poppy Seed Shortbread Bars

1/2 cup unsalted butter, softened

1/2 cup confectioners' sugar

1 1/2 tablespoons grated lemon zest

3/4 teaspoon vanilla extract

1 cup flour

1 1/2 tablespoons poppy seeds

1/2 teaspoon salt

Confectioners' sugar

Beat the butter and 1/2 cup confectioners' sugar in a mixer bowl until light and fluffy. Add the lemon zest and vanilla, beating until mixed. Add the flour, poppy seeds and salt. Beat just until combined. Press into a buttered 8-inch baking pan. Bake at 325 degrees for 15 to 20 minutes or until pale golden brown. Cool in pan on a wire rack for 10 minutes. Cut into 24 bars. Let stand in pan until completely cool. Sprinkle with additional confectioners' sugar.

Yield: 24 bars

Famous Chocolate Fudge Sauce

Add almond flavoring or amaretto. This makes a wonderful filling for tart shells, or use for a fondue.

7 ounces unsweetened
    chocolate
1³/4 cups sugar
1 tablespoon butter
¹/4 teaspoon salt
1 (12-ounce) can evaporated
    milk
1 teaspoon vanilla extract

Melt the chocolate in a double boiler over hot water. Add the sugar, butter and salt, stirring until the mixture is smooth. Add the evaporated milk. Cook until thickened, stirring frequently. Remove from the heat. Stir in the vanilla. Serve warm. May cook in the microwave in a large glass bowl on High for 3¹/2 to 4 minutes, stirring 3 to 4 times during cooking.

Yield: 4 cups

Caramel Pecan Sauce

5 tablespoons dark brown
    sugar
¹/4 cup butter
5 tablespoons cream
¹/2 cup chopped toasted
    pecans

Combine the sugar, butter and cream in a heavy saucepan. Cook over low heat for 3 to 4 minutes, stirring frequently. Remove from the heat and let stand to cool. Fold in the pecans. Serve as a sauce for pumpkin pie or various ice creams and cake.

Yield: 1 cup

Rose

The fragrant aroma and delicate, slightly sweet flavor of the rose petal is a lovely touch in salads, jams, sorbets, syrups, and ice cream.

Appendix

Getting Organized for a Party

Don't take anything for granted.

Send out invitations 2 to 3 weeks in advance of the party. People get busy during the holidays.

Make sure the room is cool before the party starts, even in winter.

Move big, cumbersome furniture out of the way along with anything fragile.

Set up the bar away from the entrance if possible and allow for plenty of room in front and to the sides of it. Never put a bar or food table at the end of a long room or in a place where there is only one way in or out. This will eliminate bottlenecks.

Cover the bar with a floor-length cloth so you can store extra glasses and what-not out of the way under it.

Introduce guests to each other.

Start serving hot hors d'oeuvres when 8 or so guests have arrived.
Replace hot hors d'oeuvres frequently.

You can rent almost anything you don't have.
Make sure you see what you are renting before you order it.

Don't forget about a place to put coats. If your bed won't do the trick, rent coat racks.

Planning an Appetizer Buffet

Bar Basics

The caterer's rule of thumb on beverages is 1 to 1½ drinks per hour per guest. If you're in a quandary about how much to buy, ask your beverage store if you can return any unopened bottles. It has been noted that people are drinking less alcohol now, so you'll likely need more wine, bottled waters, and soft drinks than you may expect and less hard liquor.

A bar with wine, beer, and mineral water is adequate for most groups. Keep food and beverage tables separated for traffic flow.

Time has a lot do do with planning. Some caterers suggest for a two-hour party, a minimum of 12 finger food pieces per guest—ten pieces of hors d'oeuvres and two sweets. Allow 2 shrimp per person if it is served. It is very popular.

If a party is to start at 7:00 p.m., it must serve as dinner. We figure 21 bites per person. If the party starts at 8:30 or later, go light on savories and offer more sweets. Know your guests. Young people eat more than an older crowd. Guests eat more at casual parties.

Wining and Dining
Wine Guide

The pairing of good food with fine wine is one of the great pleasures of life. The rule that you drink white wine only with fish and fowl and red wine with meat no longer applies—just let your own taste and personal preference be the guide. Remember to serve light wines with lighter foods and full-bodied wines with rich foods so the food and wine will complement rather than overpower each other.

Food and Wine Pairings

Semidry White Wines such as Riesling or Gewürztraminer
Dove, quail, fish or shellfish in cream sauce
Roast turkey, duck or goose
Seafood, pasta or salad
Fish in herbed butter sauce

Dry White Wines such as Chardonnay or Chablis
Roast young game birds and waterfowl
Shellfish
Fried and grilled fish

Light Red Wines such as Beaujolais or Lambrusco
Mild game sausage
Fowl with highly seasoned stuffings
Soups and stews
Hare
Creole foods

Hearty Red Wines such as Merlot Cabernet Sauvignon
Duck and goose
Game birds
Venison, wild boar and hare

How Much for How Many

For 20 guests you will need one bar; for 50 you will need two bars. The following amounts are for 20-guest and 50-guest parties. You may choose to have more or less of some items depending on your menu.

Wines	20-Guest Party	50-Guest Party
Champagne	3 bottles	6 to 7 bottles
White Wine	3 to 4 bottles	6 to 8 bottles
Red Wine	4 to 5 bottles	11 to 12 bottles
Sparkling Water or Mineral Water	12 (10-ounce) bottles	24 (10-ounce) bottles

Wine: These estimates are based on consumption of two or three (4-ounce) glasses per person over a three-hour period with food.

Chill all white wine and Champagne for at least three hours before guests arrive. Open about two bottles of red wine 30 minutes before guests arrive. Open additional wine as needed.

Bar Set-Up for 24

Dry white wine	6 bottles	Seltzer	6 liters
Dry red wine	2 bottles	Tonic water	4 liters
Champagne or sparkling wine	6 bottles	Perrier or other mineral water	3 liters
Vodka	1 liter	Ginger ale	2 liters
Scotch	1 liter	Grapefruit juice	1 quart
Single-malt scotch	1 bottle	Cranberry juice	1 quart
Rum	1 bottle	Coca-Cola	1 liter
Kentucky straight bourbon	1 bottle		
Dry fine sherry	1 bottle	*1 bottle = 750 milliliters*	
Dry French vermouth	1 bottle	*unless otherwise specified*	

Party Supply List

Supplies	20-Guest Party	50-Guest Party
Champagne glasses (1 per person)	20	50
Wine glasses (1½ per person)	30	75
Water glasses (1 per person)	20	50
Napkins (5 per person)	100	250
8-inch plates (2 per person)	40	100
Forks (2 per per person)	40	100

*F*ood: It is hard to be precise about quantity. In general, for a two- to three-hour party you should plan on two of each kind of bite-size hors d'oeuvres per person.

For 20 people, serve two to three kinds of cold hors d'oeuvres and three to four hot; one should be low in fat, preferably vegetarian. You will need a total of 200 to 280 pieces (17 to 22 dozen).

For 50 people, serve 3 to 4 cold hors d'oeuvres and 5 to 6 hot; two should be low in fat, preferably vegetarian. You will need a total of 560 to 1000 pieces (46 to 83 dozen).

Special equipment: Corkscrews, Champagne openers, serving platters, doilies, serving utensils, baking sheets, candles, matches, trivets, flowers and/or decorations, extra lined garbage cans for recyclable and regular garbage.

Ice: Two 5-pound bags should be enough. Keep an ice chest under the bar table.

Help: You can try to do everything by yourself for a party of 20, but one bartender and one waitress/waiter will allow you much more time with your guests. You can get away with just one helper if you keep your menu simple. For 50 people, one bartender and two helpers work best.

Food Quantities for Serving 25, 50, and 100 People

Food	25 Servings	50 Servings	100 Servings
Sandwiches:			
Bread	50 slices or	100 slices or	200 slices or
	3 (1-pound) loaves	6 (1-pound) loaves	12 (1-pound) loaves
Butter	1/2 pound	3/4 to 1 pound	1 1/2 pounds
Mayonnaise	1 cup	2 to 3 cups	4 to 6 cups
Mixed Filling (meat, eggs, fish)	1 1/2 quarts	2 1/2 to 3 quarts	5 to 6 quarts
Mixed Filling (sweet fruit)	1 quart	1 3/4 to 2 quarts	2 1/2 to 4 quarts
Lettuce	1 1/2 heads	2 1/2 to 3 heads	5 to 6 heads
Meat, Poultry, or Fish:			
Wieners (beef)	6 1/2 pounds	13 pounds	25 pounds
Hamburger	9 pounds	18 pounds	35 pounds
Turkey or chicken	13 pounds	25 to 35 pounds	50 to 75 pounds
Fish, large whole (round)	13 pounds	25 pounds	50 pounds
Fish fillets or steaks	7 1/2 pounds	15 pounds	30 pounds
Salads, Casseroles:			
Potato Salad	4 1/4 quarts	2 1/4 gallons	4 1/2 gallons
Scalloped Potatoes	4 1/2 quarts or 1 (12x20-inch) pan	8 1/2 quarts	17 quarts
Spaghetti	1 1/4 gallons	2 1/2 gallons	5 gallons
Baked Beans	3/4 gallon	1 1/4 gallons	2 1/2 gallons
Jello Salad	3/4 gallon	1 1/4 gallons	2 1/2 gallons

Food	25 Servings	50 Servings	100 Servings
Ice Cream:			
Brick	3$^1/_4$ quarts	6$^1/_2$ quarts	12$^1/_2$ quarts
Bulk	2$^1/_4$ quarts	4$^1/_2$ quarts or 1$^1/_4$ gallons	9 quarts or 2$^1/_2$ gallons
Beverages:			
Coffee	$^1/_2$ pound and 1$^1/_2$ gallons water	1 pound and 3 gallons water	2 pounds and 6 gallons water
Tea	$^1/_{12}$ pound and 1$^1/_2$ gallons water	$^1/_6$ pound and 3 gallons water	$^1/_3$ pound and 6 gallons water
Lemonade	10 to 15 lemons 1$^1/_2$ gallons water	20 to 30 lemons, 3 gallons water	40 to 60 lemons, 6 gallons water
Desserts:			
Watermelon	37$^1/_2$ pounds	75 pounds	150 pounds
Cake	1 (10x12-inch) sheet cake 1$^1/_2$ (10-inch) layer cakes	1 (12x20-inch) sheet cake 3 (10-inch) layer cakes	2 (12x20-inch) sheet cakes 6 (10-inch) layer cakes
Whipping Cream	$^3/_4$ pint	1$^1/_2$ to 2 pints	3 pints

Important Temperatures to Know

Meats:

Rare Steak	125° F.
Rare Roast Beef	125° F.
Well-done Beef	165° F.
Roast Pork	170° F.
Turkey/Chicken	190° F.
Duck/Goose	190° F.

Breads:

Proofing Yeast	110° F.
Most Breads	200° F.

Wine:

Dry White	47°-54° F.
Sweet White	44°-47° F.
Young Reds	54°-60° F.
Mature Reds	59°-65° F.
Champagne	42°-45° F.

Candy:

Soft Ball	234°-240° F.
Firm Ball	244°-248° F.
Hard Ball	250°-266° F.

Index

To order additional copies of

Southern Scrumptious

How To Cater Your Own Party

write to:

Scrumptious, Inc.
4107 Indian Hills Road
Decatur, Alabama 35603

Be sure to include Your Name and Complete Address for return mail.

For one copy send:	$19.95
Plus sales tax	1.60
Plus postage and handling	3.00
Total	$24.55

[   ] Desire gift wrap.

For volume purchases call 1-256-353-1897.

Make checks payable to *Scrumptious, Inc.*

[   ] VISA   [   ] MasterCard   Exp. Date _____

Account Number _____

Signature _____

About the Author

Betty Brandon Sims majored in Foods and Nutrition at the
University of Tennessee. She has long been active in her community and
in the food business, owning Johnston Street Cafe and a very
busy catering business since 1986. She has edited regional cookbooks and
presently owns *Scrumptious, Inc.*, specializing in wedding cakes,
and teaching cooking classes. She has attended Peter Kumps' Cooking
School in New York City, Martha Stewart seminars, and the
Culinary Institute, Napa Valley, among others. She is a member of the
International Association of Cooking Professionals.
Mrs. Sims lives in Decatur, Alabama, with her husband Dr. Bill Sims.
Her family includes Libby Sims Patrick, Carl and Alex;
Sheri Sims Hofherr, Peter, Brandon and Finlay;
Bill Sims, Jr., Tara, Will and Allison;
Lisa Sims Wallace, Paul, Paul, Jr., and Sims.